Mika Ninagawa: Self-image

ごあいさつ

この度、原美術館におきまして、「蜷川実花：Self-image」展を開催する運びとなりました。

鮮烈な極彩色の写真で知られる蜷川実花は、近年、映画やミュージックビデオ、ファッションデザイナーとのコラボレーションなどへも活動の幅を広げ、独自のスタイルを貫きつつ挑戦し続ける表現者として注目を集めています。鮮烈な「蜷川カラー」とともにアイドルやモデル、花々の輝きを捉えた作品が人気を博す一方で、華やかさや幸福感と隣り合わせにある歪みや澱み、衰退の影や死の気配が写り込む作品も制作してきました。

本展では、そのような闇に目を向け、新境地を開いた『noir』シリーズ、川面に散る桜を収めた『PLANT A TREE』、そして初期から断続的に撮影しているモノクロームのセルフポートレイトを中心に展観します。「生身に近い」と作家自身が語る特別な作品群（＝セルフイメージ）を紹介するこの機会に、蜷川実花作品の新たな魅力と出会っていただけたら幸いです。

最後に、本展の開催にあたり、ご協賛・ご協力を賜りました株式会社ルミネ、ドイツ銀行グループ、ガトーフェスタ ハラダ、ペリエ ジュエ、富士フイルムイメージングシステムズ株式会社、東京リスマチック株式会社、王子エフテックス株式会社、図書印刷株式会社、渋谷慶一郎、evala、ZUMI、sonihouse、小山登美夫ギャラリー、有限会社ラッキースターの皆様に感謝申し上げます。そして、作家・蜷川実花と制作にご尽力いただいた皆様に心より御礼申し上げます。

原美術館館長　原 俊夫

Foreword

The Hara Museum of Contemporary Art is happy to present the exhibition *Mika Ninagawa: Self-image*. Known for her vibrant and brilliantly colored photographs, Ninagawa has continued to attract attention by constantly taking on new challenges, which in recent years have included cinema, music videos, and even collaborations with fashion designers, all the while maintaining a style that is uniquely her own. The open, optimistic feeling of her flowers, fashion models and pop idols depicted in vivid "Ninagawa Color" stand in stark contrast with her monochrome self-portraits which explore a darker dimension of distortion, decline, stagnation and death.

The core of the exhibition consists of Ninagawa's *noir* series, a study of darkness and shadows that broke new ground for the artist; her *PLANT A TREE* series of images of cherry blossoms scattered on the surface of rivers; and her monochrome self-portraits which she began at the start of her career and has added to intermittently ever since. Together they present a "self-image" described by Ninagawa as being "close to her raw and unguarded self".

In closing, I would like to express my deepest gratitude to the LUMINE Co., Ltd, Deutsche Bank Group, GATEAU FESTA HARADA, Perrier-Jouët, FUJIFILM Imaging Systems Co., Ltd., TOKYO Lithmatic Corporation, Oji F-Tex Co., Ltd., TOSHO Printing Co., Ltd., Keiichiro Shibuya, evala, ZUMI, sonihouse Tomio Koyama Gallery and Lucky Star Co., Ltd. for their generous sponsorship and cooperation and my heartfelt thanks to Mika Ninagawa and all those who helped put this show together.

Toshio Hara　Director, Hara Museum of Contemporary Art

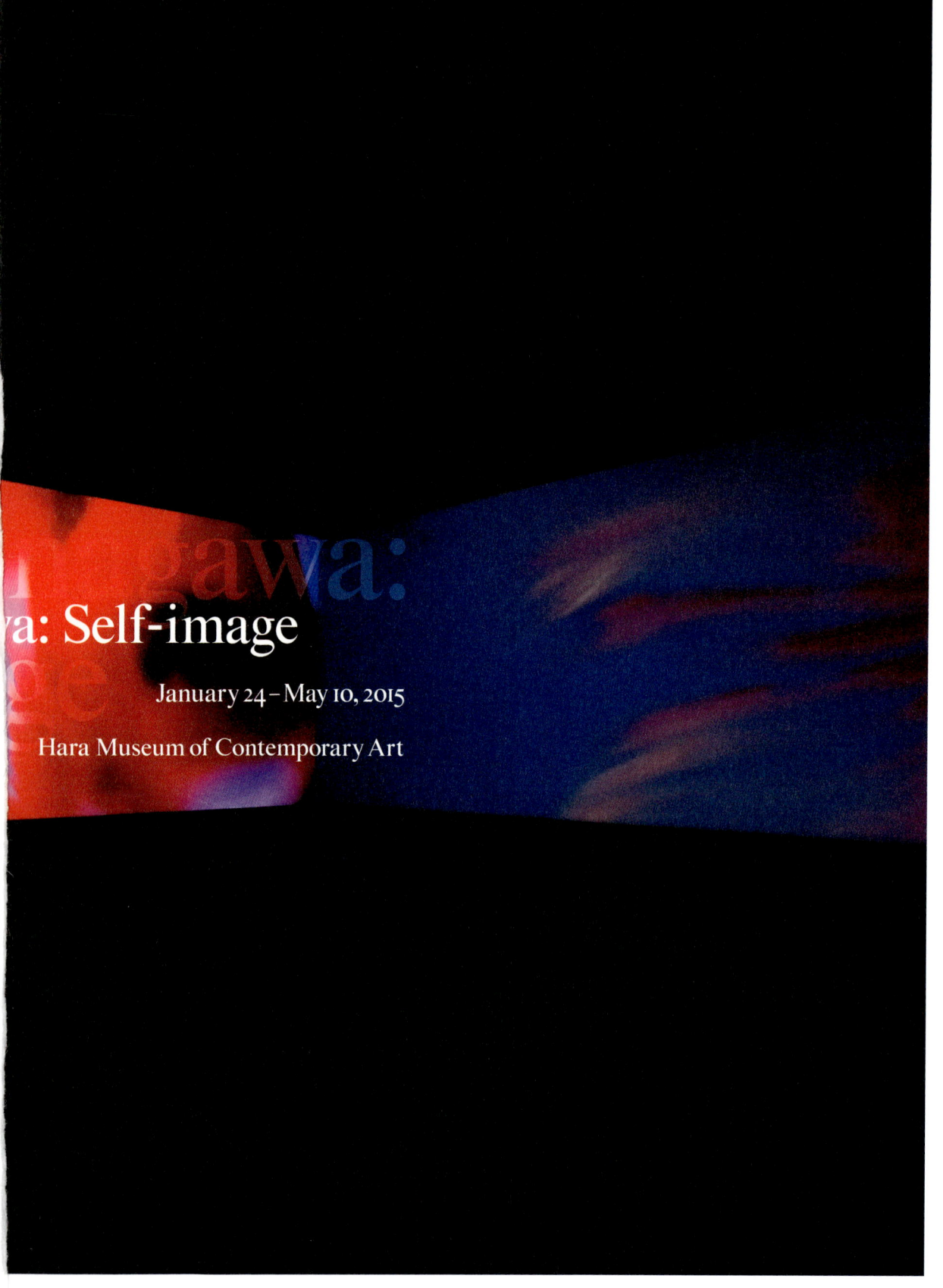

どんぐりが風で落ちる音

自分が写真をとられるのはいいのだが、写された自分をみるのは嫌だ。おそらくこれは羞恥する心の処理の問題なのだ。「セルフポートレイト」をとる写真家は、どのようにして自意識を処理しているのだろうか。

蜷川実花がとる「セルフポートレイト」には、ほとんどその種の自意識との格闘の痕跡がない。もちろん写真家が「セルフポートレイト」をとるとき、写す自分と写される自分について、なにも意識しないはずはないのだが、一枚の写真に自意識との格闘を発見するのは、みるものに、少し重いなにかを背負わせることになるのも事実だ。

蜷川実花の作品にその種の負担を感じなくてすむことに、私は少しほっとする。

暗い、少し沈んだ階調の奥からこっちをみつめている蜷川のまなざしが、何を語っているのか、その意味を知ろうとする心を私はあわてて封印をする。それは当然だ。誰が自分の娘の串ざしにされた内面をみたいだろうか。それは私にとって恐怖だ。で、私は逃走する。そのかわり私は、シャッターを切る時の一秒にもみたない瞬間を決断する、あるいは動物的な反射神経、それらを選択する力量・直感する力を、高く評価する。ほとんどこれは動物的な嗅覚といってよい才能だと思える。

私はゆるんだ写真が好きではない。私の快楽は息を詰めた一瞬にあるので、そして私が職業とする演劇もその連続だと思っているのだがたぶんゆるんでいる作品が許せないのだろう。人によってはそのことを嫌悪する人もいるがそれは仕方ないことだ。これはどのようにして世界を許容し、どのようにあらわれるその人間の本質なのだから。

今年はどんぐりが風で落ちる音がうるさい。それは庭の枯葉やベランダにあたって音をたてる。それがぼくを少しいらだたせる。私は蜷川実花の「セルフイメージ」のゲラのページを閉じる。庭の片隅に幼かった実花が遊んでいた鉄棒やブランコが風にゆれている。私はわが子の内面や肉体をそっと遠景にしようとこころみる。

蜷川幸雄[演出家]

The sound of acorns falling in the wind

Yukio Ninagawa Director (theatre)

I don't mind being photographed, but I don't like looking at photographs of myself. It's most likely to do with the way I process feelings of shame. I wonder how photographers who take portraits of themselves work through their own self-consciousness.

Self-portraits taken by Mika Ninagawa don't betray many traces of such conflict. When photographers take portraits of themselves, it's natural that they should be aware of the self that photographs and the self that is being photographed. And yet, it's also true that viewers are shouldered with a kind of weight when they look into a photograph and discover a fight in which the photographer is wrestling with self-awareness.

I'm somewhat relieved that Mika Ninagawa's work doesn't make me feel the burden of those struggles.

I close off my heart in a hurry when it tries to learn the meaning behind Ninagawa's gaze, which peers out from the depths of a dark gradation dampened by shadow. It stands to reason: who would want to see the internal life of their daughter, pierced through? That is something that I fear, something from which I run. Instead, I recognize her intuition and the caliber of her ability to choose among fractions of a second. It might also be a biological impulse or reflex that allows her to decide on the exact moment to press the shutter button. I think it's safe to say that her talent approaches a natural, animal instinct.

I don't like loose photography. My pleasure resides in moments of held breath. Drama, where I've found my occupation, is also a succession of those tense, fleeting instants, and that's probably why I have no patience for loose or relaxed work. No doubt some will think this repugnant, but that's not something I can help. People reveal their essence in the way they accept the world and how they attempt to reconcile themselves with it.

This year, the acorns falling in the wind are making a racket. They make a noise when they hit the balcony or the dead leaves in the yard. I find this a little irritating. I close the pages of a galley proof for Mika Ninagawa's *Self-image*. Swaying in the wind in one corner of the yard are the bars and swing-set with which Mika used to play when she was little. I try to push my child's internal world and bodily flesh gently into the distant background.

モノクローム・ポップ——蜷川実花の現在[1]

清水 穣［美術評論家］

　写真のモダニズムとは、あるがまま、素のままの世界、裸で純粋で無垢の存在を信じることである。写真はそのような存在を現前させるものであり、従って無我無作為、透明にして自然でなければならない。正しいイメージなどはない、ただイメージがあるだけだ、と。作らず飾らず淡々と過ぎゆく「日常」は、こうして写真の近代にとって特権的な主題となった。ラルティーグやアジェが（本当に彼らの写真がそうであるかは別として）「自然」体の写真の代表として賞賛されるのも、アマチュア写真の失敗や不器用こそが評価されるのも、「日常」といえば必ず下町のプロレタリアートの日常なのも、すべてモダンな信仰心に由来する。

　無垢で素のままの世界とは、一般的な価値観や理念や感性に汚されていない世界であり、そういう一般社会から見た「外部」である。しばしばそれは「天然の」「子供のように」「未分化で」「しなやかな」「理性的思考を絶えずすり抜けていく」「女性特有の」存在として形容される。つまりモダンな「外部」とは、成人男性の眼差しに映る「外部」であり（生物学的性別に関わらず）男のディスクールに属していると言える。一方に硬直化した男たちの既成の社会システム、他方に女子供と非・近代人による未分化で豊かな混沌があって、芸術とは、写真とは、前者を後者のなかへ解き放つことなのだ、と。

　ここで荒木経惟の最初期写真集『さっちんとマー坊』(1962)を召喚しよう。東京三河島の古い団地でスナップした作品集には、あえて期限切れカラーフィルム[2]を用いた黄昏の色調で、「労働者階級」の「子供」の「日常」が写されている。モダニストの優等生が作り込んだ写真集ということだ。しかしその後『センチメンタルな旅』(1971)までの9年間の間に、荒木は嘘がつけなくなる。一般に60年代末から70年代を通してのこの期間は、写真というメディウムが一つの断層を通過する時期である。「あるがまま」の「自然」は、最も強力なキャッチコピーとして広告資本に収奪されていき、あの信仰も弱体化していった。「外部」、つまりナチュラルで、ピュアで、リアルなものとは、もはや「新商品」に他ならない。資本の流動が「外部」を吸いつくした世界で「あるがまま」は写真に写せない、自然で純粋な現実こそは広告化した現代の大嘘なのであり、そんな「嘘写真」（『センチメンタルな旅』序言）は耐え難い、と、写真のモダニストが理解し、それでも信仰を捨てられないときどうするか。せめて写真に嘘をつかせないため、「あるがまま」の存在を嘘で汚さないために、彼は自ら「これは嘘だ」と分かる写真を撮る。最後のモダニストとなって、「不自然だぞ」「不純だぞ」「作為だぞ」と見せつける写真をわざと撮るのだ。「あるがまま」への信仰を留保するための「人工的なわざとらしさ」——「センチメンタル」とはそういうことである。

　信じるものがもはや不可能であるが故に信仰を捨てないという、最後のモダニストタイプの写真家は日本に少なくない。その彼らが90年代に入って「女の子写真」を評価するに到る。それは文字通り「日本の（＝エキゾチック）女（＝非・近代人）」の「日常」を写した「アマチュア写真」であった。若くて「天然」で「ぶっ飛んだ」「素顔」の女性作家たちが、日常のなかのリアルな瞬間を、いま・ここで写し留めた写真群。中高年のモダニストたちにとって、素人丸出し、ピントも甘く、ボケたヘタウマ作品は、昔の夢がカラフルに蘇ったようなものであったろう。ああ俺たちは、生のリアルな存在を「ドキュメント」したくて、カメラを傾けピントを呆けさせ、画面をブレさせプリントを荒れさせたものだなあ。「あるがままに」——それは不可能ではあったけど、写真の本質はやっぱりそこだよ。自分たちがやれば古臭いけど、女の子がやるのはいいじゃない。いまどき素直さは貴重だよ。その点、男は考え過ぎちゃうからダメだけど、いいなあ、女は過激で自由で。

　「バ～カ」と、蜷川実花が思ったか思わなかったか。彼女がデビューしたのは、モダンなディスクールに相変わらず支配された環境であった。2000年度第26回木村伊兵衛写真賞（もちろん選考委員は全員男：篠山紀信、都築響一、藤原新也、廣瀬弘、高梨豊）は、

オヤジ達のこのような夢を投影された「女の子御三家」、HIROMIX、長島有里枝そして蜷川実花が受賞した。流行の締めくくりのように、というのも、オヤジの夢 ——バブルの残響—— はその後すぐに薄れ、ほとんどの「女の子」作家もきれいに忘れられていったのであり、本当に木村友紀、米田知子、春木麻衣子、笹岡啓子、頭山ゆう紀…といった女性作家達が頭角を現すのは、「女の子写真」が消えた後の時代だった。

*

さて、上記の60〜70年代にかけての時期、当然ながら多くの作家達は「写真」について根本的な再考を迫られた。行き詰まった白黒ストレート写真の代わりに、「カラー」がオルターナティヴな表現手段として再発見され、コンセプト・フォト ——写真についての写真—— が現れるのもこの時期である。荒木経惟の「センチメンタル」もその一例と見なせるが、この時期、「ナチュラル」「リアル」「あるがまま」といった価値に対して批評的に関わる態度が、2つ現れる。1つは「キャンプ」、もうひとつは「ポップ」である。「カラー」「キャンプ」そして「ポップ」——これらが蜷川実花を理解する3つの鍵である。

「カラー」は、とくに最後のモダニストたちにとって興味深い位置を占めている。システム（文化的諸価値の網目に覆われた世界）とその外部（網目の外のあるがままの世界）という2つの対立項を立て、前者を後者へ導くのが写真だとするモダニズムにとって、「カラー」は絵画的伝統に属し、「あるがまま」「裸」の世界にかけられた虚飾として排除の対象であった。つまりモダニストにとって「カラー」は最も明白な「嘘」である。だから最後のモダニストたちにとって「カラー」は、それが鮮やかであればあるほど、「あるがまま」への信仰を留保するための「人工的なわざとらしさ」にもっとも相応しい表現手段となった。

「キャンプ」については、スーザン・ソンタグがいち早く同時代的に論じた文章[3]が知られている。キャンプとは、広告資本が求めた「外部」的価値、例えば「リアルな女」を、大真面目にそして装飾過剰に演出してみせることによって、それを宙吊りにする態度である。他にも「あるがまま」「自然」「リアル」…をやり過ぎるまで自作自演する、つまり60年代後半に荒木経惟が耐えられなくなった「嘘写真」をそのまま楽しむスタイルである。1976年に北島敬三らによって開設された自主ギャラリー「CAMP」がその流れを受けていることは言うまでもない。そしてその北島の『NEW YORK』(1982) は、路上の「リアル」を「ドキュメント」するスタイルを網羅的に、そして過剰に使い尽くしてみせる、いわば前世代「プロヴォーク」のドラグ・クイーン的な=批評的な表現であった。

*

さて、蜷川実花と言えば、まさしく「カラー」である。12年前、彼女の写真について私は次のように書いた：

…蜷川実花『17 9 '97』（メタローグ1998年）『ピンク・ローズ・スウィート』（エディシオン・トレヴィル2001年）には、下手なスナップ写真の勢いが充溢している。綺麗な色が好き、だから色を撮る、それだけ。たっぷりと流れ落ちるような色彩と、ノンシャランな下手ぶりがよくマッチして写真の単純な面白さが発揮される。同じように色を撮っているのに丁寧な作りで写真のうまい佐内正史が、いきなりダサく見えて来るではないか。つまりその面白さは、上手い写真家が当て馬になるからこそ味わえる類のものであって、懐石ばかりじゃなくてたまにはピッツァ！という感じではある。

「批評の不在、写真の過剰 —— 1990年代以降の現代写真とティルマンス」
『BT 美術手帖』2002年4月号

割烹佐内ではなくピッツェリア実花の、生地に好きなものを載せて薪窯で焼いただけのピッツァが、私にとっての蜷川作品だったわけである。

その認識を改めるきっかけが、2003年、グラーツで開催され、蜷川実花も参加した現代日本写真展[4]での出来事であった。あるドイツのギャラリストから、蜷川実花にインタビューしたいので通訳してほしいと頼まれた私は、そこで初めて彼女を知った。彼の質問は、同じく出展者であった澤田知子ならば即答できたであろう質問、すなわち特殊な国「ニッポン」の「女」と写真をめぐる質問であった。つまりそのドイツ人は、ニッポンの「女の子写真」の代表（とされていた）蜷川実花の写真に、ゴーギャンがタヒチの女に見たような、豊潤なカオスや女性性を認めようとしたのだが、その意図を察知した蜷川はそのことごとくを否定し、「女の子写真」というくくりも拒絶し、さらに木村伊兵衛賞の選考に対しても不快感を示した。お馴染みの質疑応答パターンの通訳で良いだろう、と高をくくっていた私は驚いてしまった。ノンシャランな色彩？とんでもない。彼女の発言をドイツ語に訳すたびにインタビュアーの顔に困惑が広がるのを眺めながら、私は蜷川実花の美しくも誇張した色彩は、ドラァグクイーンの化粧なのではないかと思い始めたのである。北島敬三が「リアル」「ドキュメンタリー」スタイルを消尽したように、蜷川実花は「カラー」を蕩尽している、「センチメンタル」に対して「キャンプ」で抵抗しているのではないか、と。

蜷川の初監督作品『さくらん』(2007)は、男の夢に合わせて形成された世界、吉原のなかで、男の欲望の対象に過激になりきることによって出世し、最後にはそこから抜け出していく花魁の話であった。これを写真の文脈に翻訳すると、男の夢に合わせて形成された世界（＝写真のモダニズム）のなかで、男（＝センチメンタルな中高年モダニスト）の欲望の対象（＝カラー）に過激になりきること（＝キャンプ）によって出世し、最後にはそこから出ていく、となるだろう。蜷川実花が出ていった先は「ポップ」である。キャンプとポップはどう違うか。「ポップアートは、たんなるキャンプではない場合には、それと関係はあるにしてもやはり非常に異なった態度を表現している。ポップアートのほうが平板で乾いており、真面目であり、ディタッチメントを保っており、究極においてニヒリスティック[5]である。」キャンプは、オヤジの夢を誇張し、その滑稽さを笑いはするが、否定することなく付き合ってやる。しかしポップとは夢を見ないことなのだ。カラフルな夢に、初めから付き合わないのである。

*

蜷川実花を理解する3つ目のキーワード、「ポップ」とは、「いま・ここ」「リアル」「あるがまま」といった一回性・真正性を、機械的反復という手段で脱構築するものである。かつてのポップアートは、「リアル」そのものが消費社会の究極の商品と化した状況に反応した最初のアートであった。ここで篠山紀信を召喚しよう。写真史における上記の断層に篠山もまた無自覚だったはずはない。ただ、もともとそんなモダンなイデオロギーに感染していなかった彼は、「リアル」が失墜したとき、リアルを留保したままフェイクをフェイクするという方法的倒錯 ──杉本博司や荒木経惟── をとる必要がなかったし[6]、フェイクと成り果てたリアルの、その嘘臭さこそを笑って許すといったキャンプな耽美主義とも無縁であった。リキテンステインがそうであったように、彼は「リアル」だの「ナチュラル」だのに連なってきたあらゆる写真を、漫画のような消費財と見なしてき使ったのである。彼の写真にはモダンな巨匠達のスタイルがあからさまに、いやひょっとしたら本人達よりも巧く使われている。使える写真はみな使え。乾いた「ポップ」に相応しく、巨匠達のスタイルを優れた写真技巧で複製することを通じて、篠山はそこに含まれた「リアル」という「夢」の湿気を蒸発させる。そうして作り込まれた篠山写真は、ファインダーを覗くこの目玉以外はすべてレディメイドの写真であるという状況 ──夢のない＝あるがままでもリアルでもない、雑色で不純なただの日々── を肯定するのである。ドキュメンタリーを陽干しにする篠山紀信の『晴れた日』は、写真集を開く者の前に1974年の日本をそのような日々として蘇らせる。

蜷川実花の『noir』(2010)を見た時、特にその沈み込む濃厚な色調に、私は『晴れた日』を思い出した。「キャンプ」の果てで、蜷川実花は「ポップ」を追いかけ、篠山紀信のお株を奪おうとしているようにすら見える。近年の蜷川写真に顕著なことは、特定の写真のスタイルやモチーフ、とりわけ森山大道（『にっぽん劇場写真帖』『狩人』のモチーフやインスタレーション、大道モノクロ写真の様々なトーン）と篠山紀信（芸能人をオブジェとしてキッチュな色使いで撮影するスタイル）の参照なのだ。だが『晴れた日』が輪島功一、長嶋茂雄、山口百恵など時代のアイコンを外さない点で、ほとんど古典的な明確さを帯びているのとは対照的に、蜷川ポップにはそのような明確なアイコンがない。森山や篠山などポストモダン第一世代の巨匠達のスタイルを、蜷川カラーのなかで反復することを通じて、彼女は何をしているのだろうか。

　二作目の映画『ヘルタースケルター』(2012)は岡崎京子の原作(2003)に基づく。男女を問わず誰もが「美しい」「カワイイ」と見なす理想のモデル体型を、「骨と目ん玉と髪と耳とあそこ以外」全てを整形することで実現したヒロインのりりこは、その事実を曝露されたスキャンダルの最中に、片方の眼球を抉り捨てて芸能界から蒸発したが、メキシコのフリークショーでどっこい生き延びていた（?）という話である。誰もが「美しい」と見なすスタイル（＝蜷川カラー）を、整形（＝スタイルやモチーフの複製＋反復）で実現した写真家…「ヘルタースケルター」は、「キャンプ」で耽美な世界から出ていくために蜷川実花が投げ捨てた片眼だったのだろう。そして一眼レフのように片眼になった彼女が、ポップな写真家としてあらためて「自己」を見つめ、リミックスしたものが本展なのである。311以後の日本の、夢のないただの日々を肯定すること、「私はこの不感症の日々を精一杯生きる」という『noir』の最後の言葉は、ポップ写真家の最初の一言にこそ相応しい。その最初の一言が、「精一杯の日々を生きる」作家の「セルフイメージ」となって反復されている。

(1) この小論は2012年『ユリイカ』7月号（青土社）の蜷川実花特集に寄せた蜷川論「キャンプの果て――蜷川実花の変容」に加筆したものです。

(2) 「あるがまま」の世界を表現するには、作家個人の絵作りの技巧は最低限に留めるべきであるから、暗室を使わないレディメイドプリントのカラー写真は、作者不介入という意味でモダニズムの倫理と矛盾しない。期限切れカラーフィルムとは、作者不介入に加えてもはや生産者ですら不介入ということで、優等生荒木の念入りさが伺える。

(3) 《キャンプ》についてのノート」(1964年)。スーザン・ソンタグ『反解釈』（高橋康也ほか訳、ちくま学芸文庫）所収。

(4) *Keep in Touch. Positions in Japanese Photography* Kunsthaus Graz, 2003年

(5) ソンタグ前掲書460頁。

(6) 『決闘写真論』(1977年)において、中平卓馬が篠山紀信に大いなる健康を見たのはそのためである。篠山紀信が、荒木経惟の亡くなった妻の写真に激怒したのは、荒木のシアトリカリティがその影にリアルへの信仰を留保していたことに気がついたからである。

Monochrome Pop: The Recent Works of Mika Ninagawa[1]

Minoru Shimizu Art critic

"Modernist" photography places its faith in the world "as it is," in an unadulterated world and an existence that is naked, pure and innocent. Because photography brings this existence to the fore, it must be natural, transparent and spontaneous. As Jean-Luc Godard said: "Ce n'est pas une image juste, c'est juste une image." ("This is not a just image, it is just an image.") And so the unpretentious, matter-of-fact and quotidian become the privileged motifs. As a result of this modernist faith, Lartigue's and Atget's photographs are praised as "natural" (whether they are actually natural being beside the point), amateur works are celebrated precisely for their defects and clumsiness, and the "quotidian" must be of the downtown proletarian kind.

An unadulterated and pure world is one unsullied by conventional values, beliefs and sensibilities. In the eyes of general society, it is an "external" world often described with such words as "undifferentiated," "tabula rasa," "supple," "free from the restraints of rational thinking" and "feminine." One might say that the modernist external is the version reflected in the eyes of adult males, one that belongs to a male discourse (unrelated to biological distinctions). From this perspective, there is the rigid preexisting social system of males on one hand, and the rich, undifferentiated chaos of women, children and non-modern peoples on the other. Art and photography are the release of the former into the latter.

Here I call upon *Satchin and Mabo* (1962), Nobuyoshi Araki's first book of photos. This collection of snapshots taken at an old apartment complex in Mikawashima, Tokyo, shows the daily lives of children of working class people captured in yellow hues on expired film.[2] That is to say, it is a book of photos crafted by a star pupil of modernist photography. However, during the nine years leading up to his next book, *Sentimental Journey* (1971), Araki would stop telling lies. From the end of the '60s through the '70s, a fault line opened up in the medium of photography: the "naturalness" of the world "as it is" was co-opted and turned into advertising capital and powerful catch copy as the faith in that world became weaker. The "external," i.e., the natural, pure and real, were now nothing more than "new products." The "external" had been absorbed by capital flows, rendering the world "as it is" impossible to capture as a photograph. What is the modernist photographer to do when all that was real, natural and pure has become the modern big lie that is advertising, when "lying photographs" (as mentioned in the foreword to *Sentimental Journey*) are no longer bearable, and yet despite this he or she is still unable to abandon the faith? They protect existence "as it is" from being defiled by those lies in the first place by taking photos that announce to the viewer that "this is a lie." Becoming a last modernist, Araki began to take photos that were manifestly "not natural," "not pure" and "fabricated." In other words, the notion behind "*Sentimental*" Journey was the use of "contrivance" to preserve faith in the world "as it is."

Japan has no lack of this last modernist-type of photographer who has not abandoned faith for the very reason that faith is no longer tenable. Entering the '90s, the so-called "girl photos" were now something they could appreciate. These are "amateurish" works showing the "everyday lives" of Japanese (= exotic) girls (=non-modern people). The photographers were young, "natural", "outre" and "guileless" women who captured real quotidian moments in the "here and now." Their amateurish, blurry or out-of-focus, bad-but-charming photos probably appeared to the middle-aged and older modernists like old bygone dreams resurrected in dazzling colors. They probably thought how nice it is to be able to "document" raw and real existence with tipped camera, bad focusing, shaky grip and grainy printing. Photographing the world "as it is": this was something they could not do, even if it was admittedly the essence of the photo. If they tried, it would seem old-fashioned. So it's great girls are doing it. Modern-day straightforwardness is important. Men are hopeless at it because they think too much. It's lucky to be a girl, to be over the top and free.

"Rubbish!" Is this what Mika Ninagawa thought about all

this? When she made her debut, the world was still in the sway of the modernist discourse. In 2000, the 26th Kimura Ihei Award (the selection panel – Kishin Shinoyama, Kyoichi Tsuzuki, Shinya Fujiwara, Hiroshi Hirose, Yutaka Takanashi – were all men, of course) was shared by three women: HIROMIX, Yurie Nagashima and Mika Ninagawa – the "Big Three" of girl photographers upon whom the dream was projected. But like a fad, the middle-aged male's dream – the echo of the bubble – grew feeble immediately afterwards and the "girl" artists were nearly completely forgotten. In fact, for such female artists as Yuki Kimura, Tomoko Yoneda, Maiko Haruki, Keiko Sasaoka and Yuuki Touyama, their era began right after the disappearance of the "girl photos."

*

During the period in question, the 60s to the 70s, many artists were naturally being compelled to reconsider "photography" in a fundamental way. This period brought forth the conceptual photograph (i.e., photos about photos) and the rediscovery of color as an alternative to straight monochrome photography that had reached its limits. Araki's *Sentimental Journey* can be considered one example of these trends. This period also saw the appearance of two critical attitudes toward such qualities as "natural," "real" and "as it is." One was "Camp" and the other was "Pop." Color, Camp and Pop – these are the three keys to understanding Mika Ningagawa.

For the last modernists, color occupies an interesting position. For them, two opposing terms are posited: the system (comprising a world covered with a mesh of cultural values) and the external (the world "as it is" lying outside of the mesh). What guides the former into the latter is photography. For a modernist, color belongs to the pictorial tradition of painting, which as an ostentation applied onto the "naked" world "as is," and was thus targeted for removal. It was, in other words, the most obvious "lie." For the last modernists then, the most appropriate means of expressing the "artificial contrivance" that would preserve faith in the world "as it is" would be color, the more vivid the better.

Written during this same period, Susan Sontag's early essay about Camp[3] is well known. Camp is an attitude by which the "external" values coveted by advertising capital, such as "real women," are displayed in such an overtly ostentatious and earnest manner that all judgment on them is placed in a state of suspension. It is also the presentation of the world "as it is," the "natural" and the "real" in an over-the-top manner. That is to say, Camp is a style that relishes the "lying" photographs that Nobuyoshi Araki found unbearable during the latter half of the '60s. Needless to say, this was the trend adopted by CAMP, the independent gallery started by Keizo Kitajima and others in 1976. In his book *NEW YORK* (1982), Kitajima's style was to "document" the "real" in an obviously exhaustive and excessive manner; that is to say, a drag queen (i.e., critical) version of the *Provoke* style that came before.

*

Mention Mika Ninagawa and one undoubtedly thinks of color. I wrote the following about her photographs 12 years ago:

... Mika Ninagawa's *17 9 '97* (Metalogue, 1998) or *Pink Rose Suite* (Éditions Treville, 2001) contains the exuberant power of the unskilled snapshot. She likes pretty colors and photographs pretty colors. That's all. Lots of color, colors that look almost fluid-like, well matched with a nonchalant absence of skill that imbue the picture with a simple fascination. Suddenly a skilled photographer like Masafumi Sanai, who also photographs colors but in a meticulously crafted way, seems uncool. It's a fascination that arises from the contrast with a photographer of great skill, in the way someone who eats at renowned Japanese restaurants all the time sometimes only wants to eat pizza!

[Excerpted from *Hihyou no fuzai, shashin no kajo - 1990 nendai ikou no gendai shashin to Tillmans* (*An Absence of Criticism, an Excess of Photos—Wolfgang Tillmans and Contemporary Photography since the 1990s*) (BT Bijutsu Techo, April, 2002)]

For me, Ninagawa's photos are the pizza: instead of the starred restaurant Chez Sanai, this pizza was one baked at Mika's Pizzeria with all of her favorite toppings.

However, I came to a new understanding of her work by way of an exhibition of contemporary Japanese photography[4] that took place in Graz in 2003, which included Mika Ninagawa. A German gallerist wanted to interview her and I was asked to interpret. It was my first time to meet Ninagawa. His questions were the kind that could be answered immediately by someone like Tomoko Sawada, another artist in the show. That is to say, his questions were about photography and "girls" from that "exotic" place Japan. The German gallerist was attempting to read into Ninagawa's photos the rich chaos and femininity Gauguin found in Tahitian women, but Ninagawa, who had caught on to his intent, would have none of that. She refused to be encapsulated by the phrase "girl photographs" and even expressed discontent over her selection for the Kimura Ihei Award. This took me by surprise, as I had made light of the task on hand, expecting it to the typical Q&A. Nonchalant color? It's nothing of the sort. Each time I translated her words into German, I noticed growing dismay on the German interviewer's face. It was then that I began to think maybe Ninagawa's exaggerated, beautiful colors were in fact the make-up of a drag queen. Like Keizo Kitajima's exhaustive use of the "real" and the "document," I began to wonder if Ninagawa's dissipation of "color" was her "Camp" way of resisting the "sentimental."

Ninagawa's directorial debut *Sakuran* (2007) is the story of a courtesan who achieves success by radically identifying herself as an object of desire for men, but who in the end leaves that world behind. Translating this into the context of photography, we get Ninagawa achieving success in a world formed around the male dream (=modernist photography) by radically assuming the identity (=Camp) of the object of desire (=color) of men (=sentimental modernists), and then ending up leaving that world. The place where Ninagawa goes to is "Pop." What is the difference between Camp and Pop? Susan Sontag describes Pop as follows: "Pop Art, which—when it is not just Camp—embodies an attitude that is related but still very different. Pop Art is more flat and more dry, more serious, more detached, ultimately nihilistic."[5] Camp inflates the dream of the male modernist and then laughs at its ridiculousness, but continues to keep company with that dream without refuting it. Pop, however, is about not dreaming at all. From the start, it keeps no company with colorful dreams.

*

Pop, the third key to understanding Ninagawa, deconstructs the once-and-only quality and authenticity - the "here and now," the "real world" and the "world as it is" - through the use of mechanical reproduction. Pop Art was the first to respond to the extreme commercialization of the "real" by consumer society. On this point, let us call upon Kishin Shinoyama. Shinoyama would not have been unaware of the fault line in the history of photography. However, since he was never indoctrinated in modernist ideology, he had no need for the methodology of perversion of a Hiroshi Sugimoto or a Nobuyoshi Araki in which a fake of a fake is presented in order to retain the "real" at a time when that "real" has been discredited.[6] He also had nothing to do with the Camp aestheticism that simultaneously mocks the "real" that has been reduced to a fake while putting up with the smell of the lie. He blatantly incorporates, as did Lichtenstein, every kind of photograph linked to the "real" or the "natural," etc., treating them like consumer items in the way comics are. Shinoyama brazenly appropriates the styles of modern masters and applies them, often with greater skill than the masters themselves. For him, all photographs are up for grabs. In reproducing the style of the masters with impeccable photographic skill, he dehydrates the "dream" of the "real," producing works that correspond to the dryness of Pop Art. His concocted photographs confirm a state in which everything other than the eyeball looking through the finder is a ready-made photograph; a state of day-to-day life devoid of dreams, made up of dull days that are neither "real" nor the "world as is." Anyone who opens up *A Fine Day* will find such days resurrected in front of them in the form of 1974 Japan by Shinoyama, who hangs the "documentary" out to dry.

When I saw Mika Ninagawa's *noir* (2010), it reminded me of *A Fine Day*, especially the sunken, deep color tones. Having reached the end of Camp, she chases after Pop and seems to be beating Kishin Shinoyama at his own game. Conspicuous in her work of recent years are specific photographic styles and motifs, especially the motifs and installations of Daido Moriyama (*Japan, a Photo Theater II* (1978) and *A Hunter* (1972)) and Kishin Shinoyama (e.g., the shooting of celebrities as objects in kitschy colors). However, there is a contrast between the inseparable connection that exists in *A Fine Day* with such icons of the day as Koichi Wajima, Shigeo Nagashima and Momoe Yamaguchi, who bathe the book in their almost classical brilliance, and the total absence of similar icons in Mika Ninagawa. So what is she trying to do with her stylistic iterations of the first post-modern masters in Ninagawa Color?

In Ninagawa's second movie *Helter Skelter* (2012), which is based on the story by Kyoko Okazaki (2003), the heroine Liliko personifies all the attributes of beauty and cuteness which both men and women look for in the ideal model. Everything in Liliko, however, is the product of plastic surgery, except for her "bones, eyeballs, ears, hair, ears and 'you-know-what' down below." This dark secret is exposed and in the middle of the scandal, she plucks out an eyeball and disappears from the entertainment world, only to reappear (as implied by the ending) alive and well in a Mexican freak show. As a photographer who used plastic surgery (the replication and repetition of styles and motifs) to create a style considered by all to be "beautiful" (Ninagawa Color), *Helter Skelter* might be the eyeball plucked out by Mika Ninagawa in order to make her exit from the world of Camp aesthetics. Now one-eyed like a single-lens reflex camera, Ninagawa, as a Pop photographer, has taken another look at "herself" and created the remix of her works that constitutes this exhibition. The book *noir* ends with the words: "I will live every frigid day to the fullest." These last words speak of the desensitized day-to-day life without dreams that followed in the wake of 3/11, words well-suited to serve as the first words of a Pop photographer, words reiterated in the form of the "Self-image" of an artist who "lives everyday to its fullest."

(1) This essay is a revised version of an article that appeared in the July 2012 issue of the journal *Eureka* (published by Seido-sha) entitled *Extreme Camp-the Transformation of Mika Ninagawa (Camp no Hate-Ninagawa Mika no Henbo)*.

(2) Depicting the world of "as it is" necessitates the minimization of artistic skill. Since ready-made color prints do not require a darkroom, they conform well to this rule of non-intervention by the artist. Star student that he was, Araki's use of expired color film underscores his meticulous adherence to the rule by extending it to include the manufacturer of the film as well.

(3) *Notes about Camp* (1964) in Susan Sontag, *Against Interpretation* (Picador, 1966, p.292)

(4) *Keep in Touch. Positions in Japanese Photography*, Kunsthaus Graz, 2003.

(5) ibid., Susan Sontag, *Against Interpretation*, p 460.

(6) This is the reason why Takuma Nakahira, in *Duel on Photography* (1977), saw such healthy robustness in Kishin Shinoyama. Shinoyama was angry at Nobuyoshi Araki's photos of his deceased wife because he noticed a continuing faith in the "real" lurking in the shadows of his theatricality.

Mika Ninagawa
Self-image

January 24 – May 10, 2015

Hara Museum of Contemporary Art

蜷川実花が、原美術館で……。

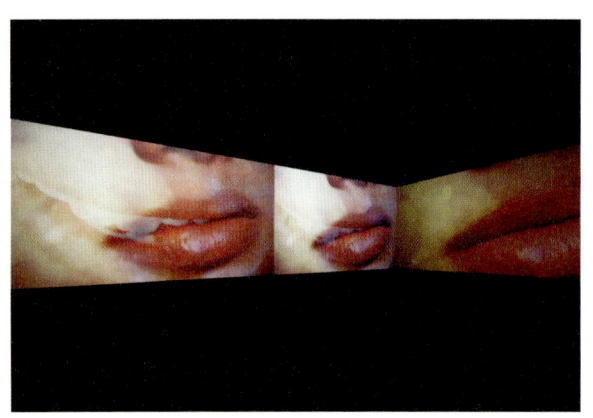

Gallery I *Gallery II*

Gallery IV

Gallery V

Window

Gallery III

Mika Ninagawa: Self-image

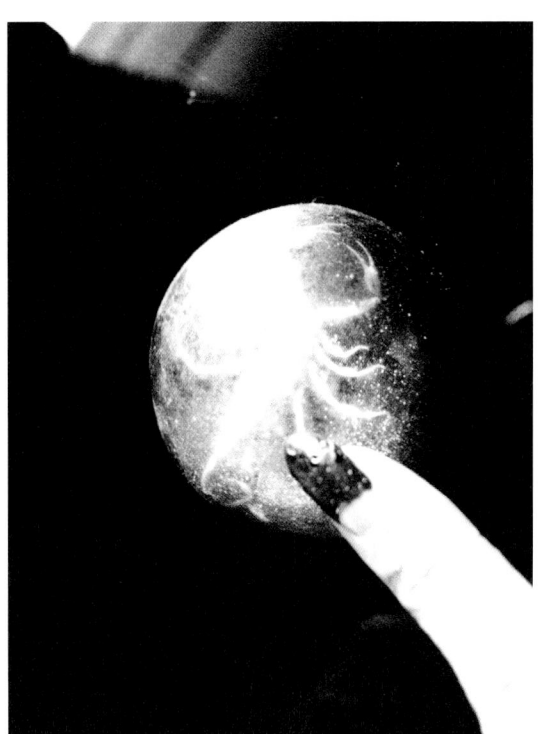

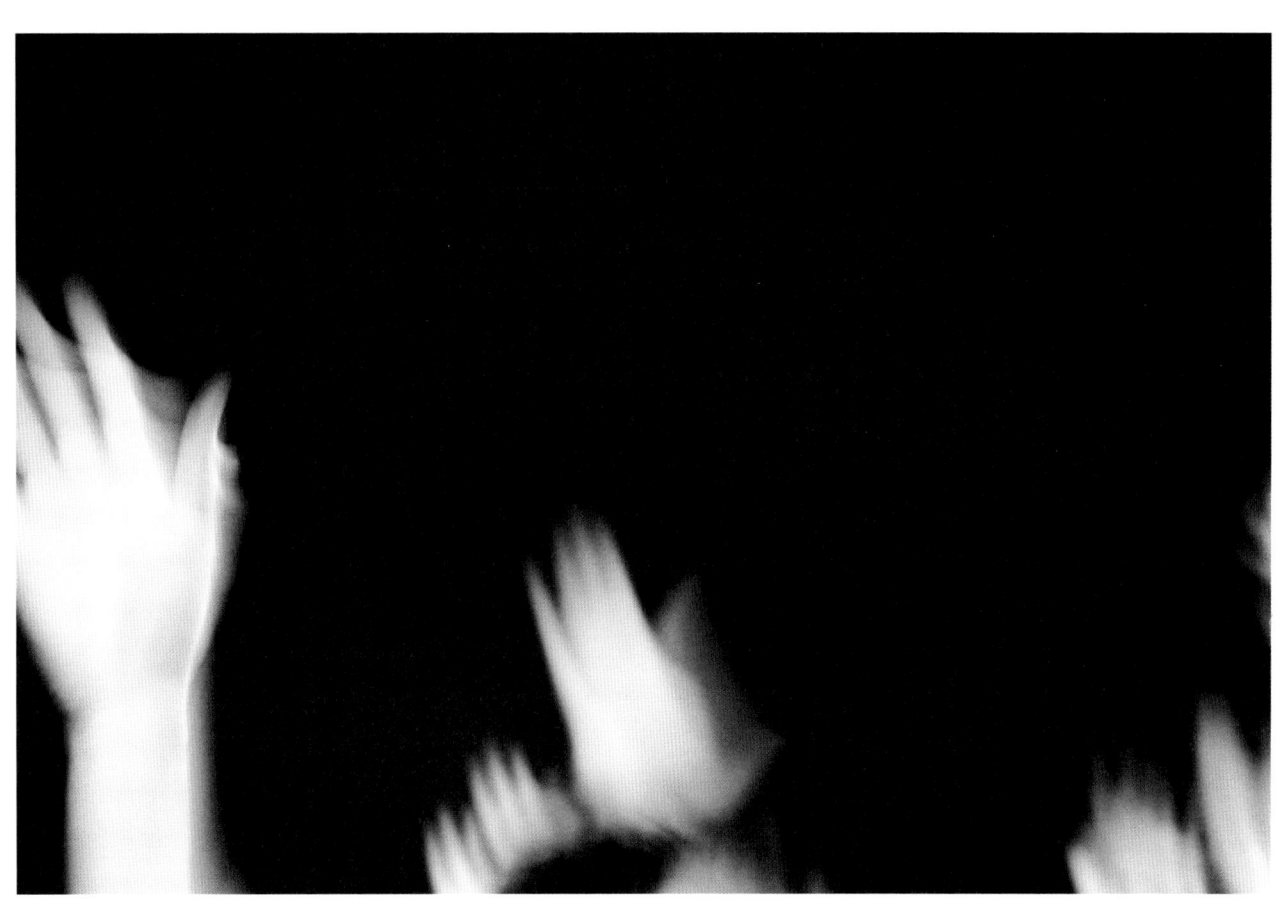

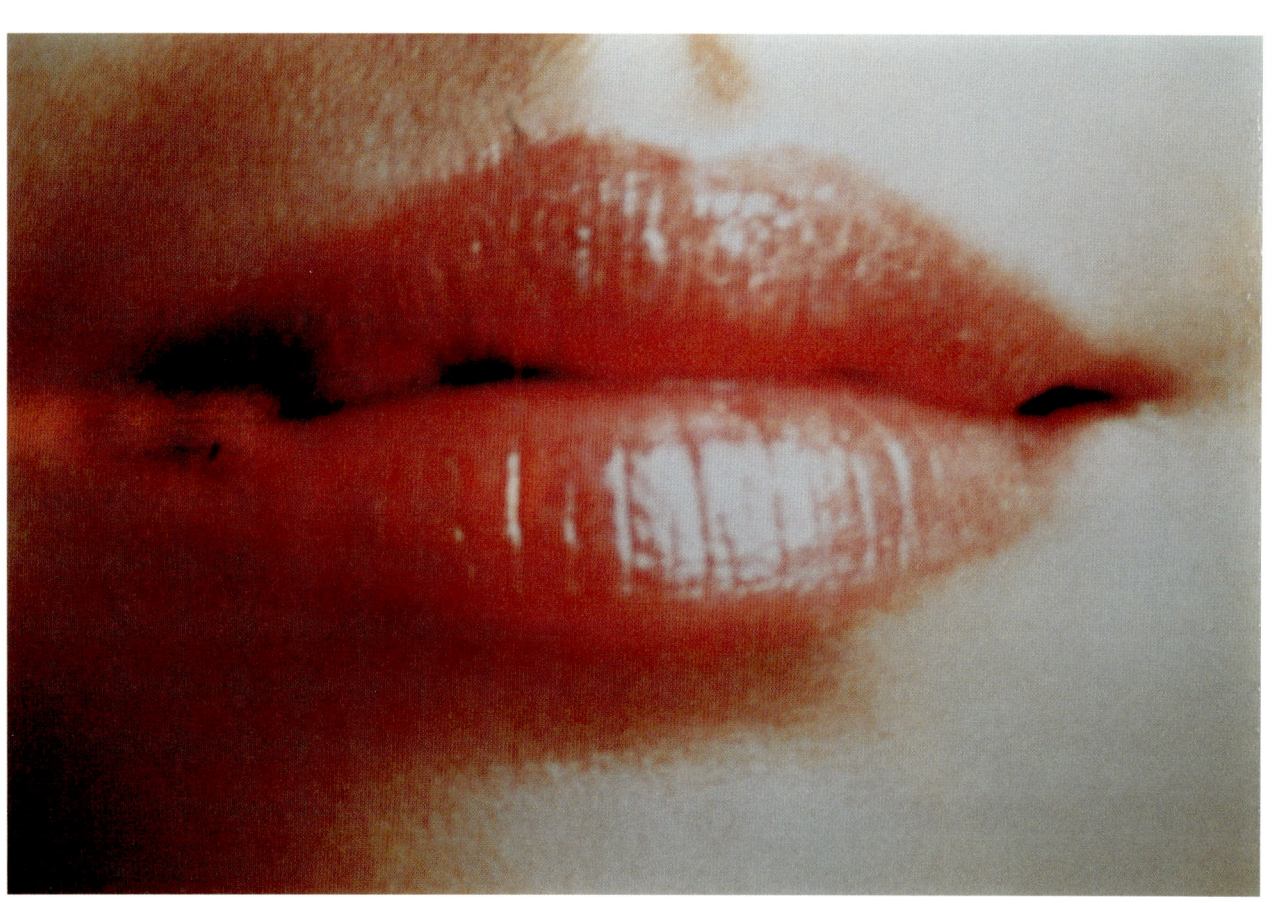

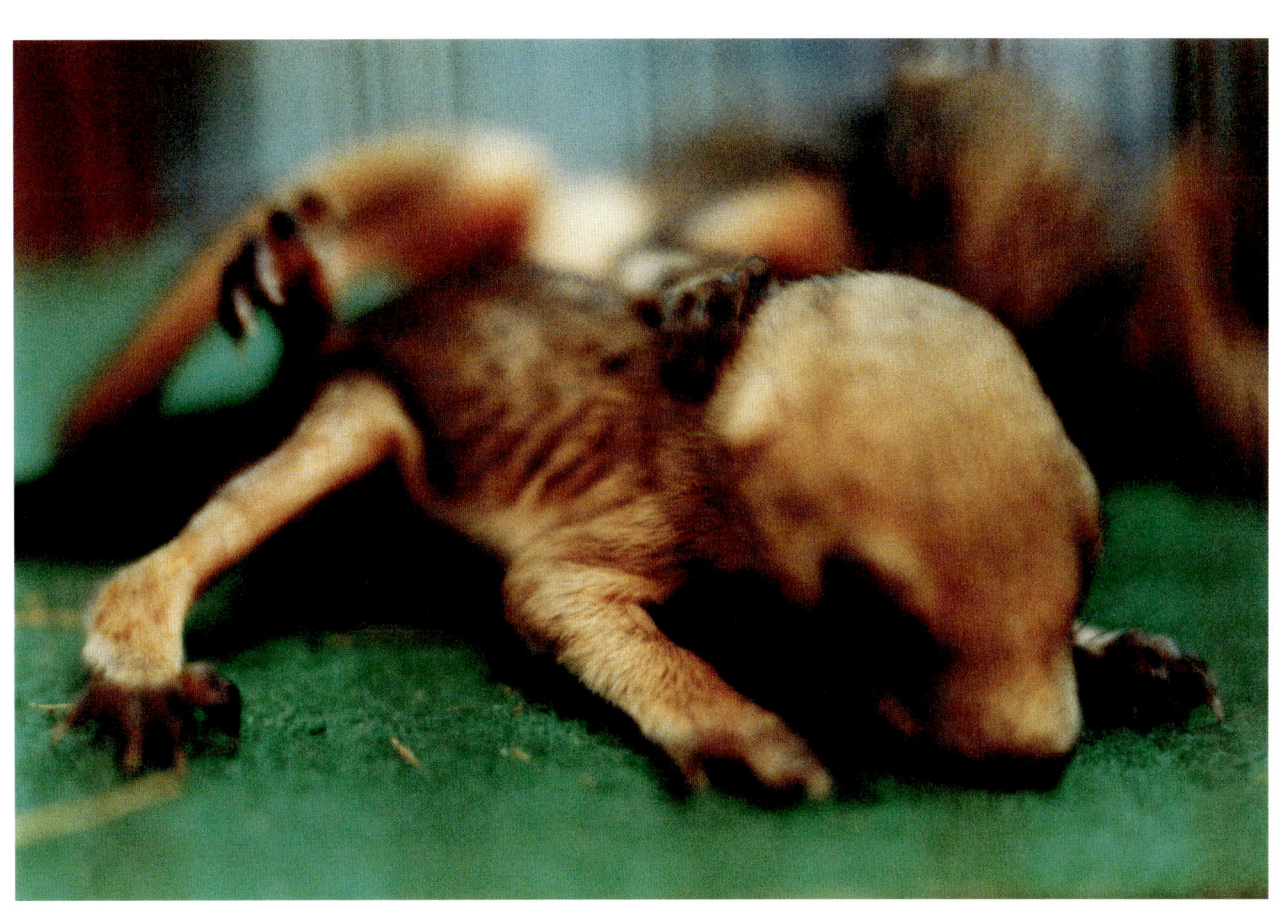

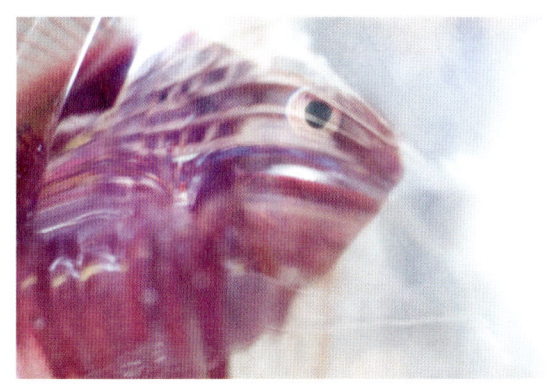

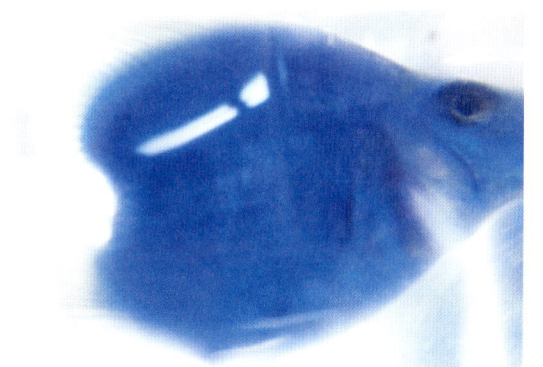
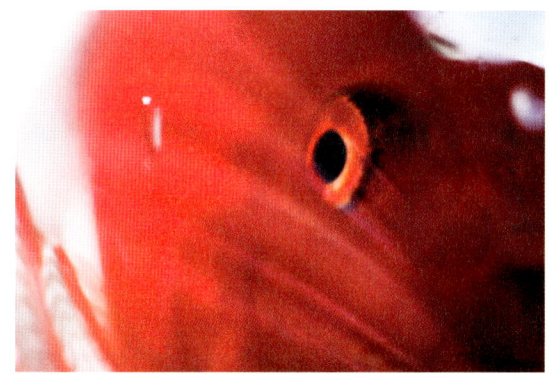

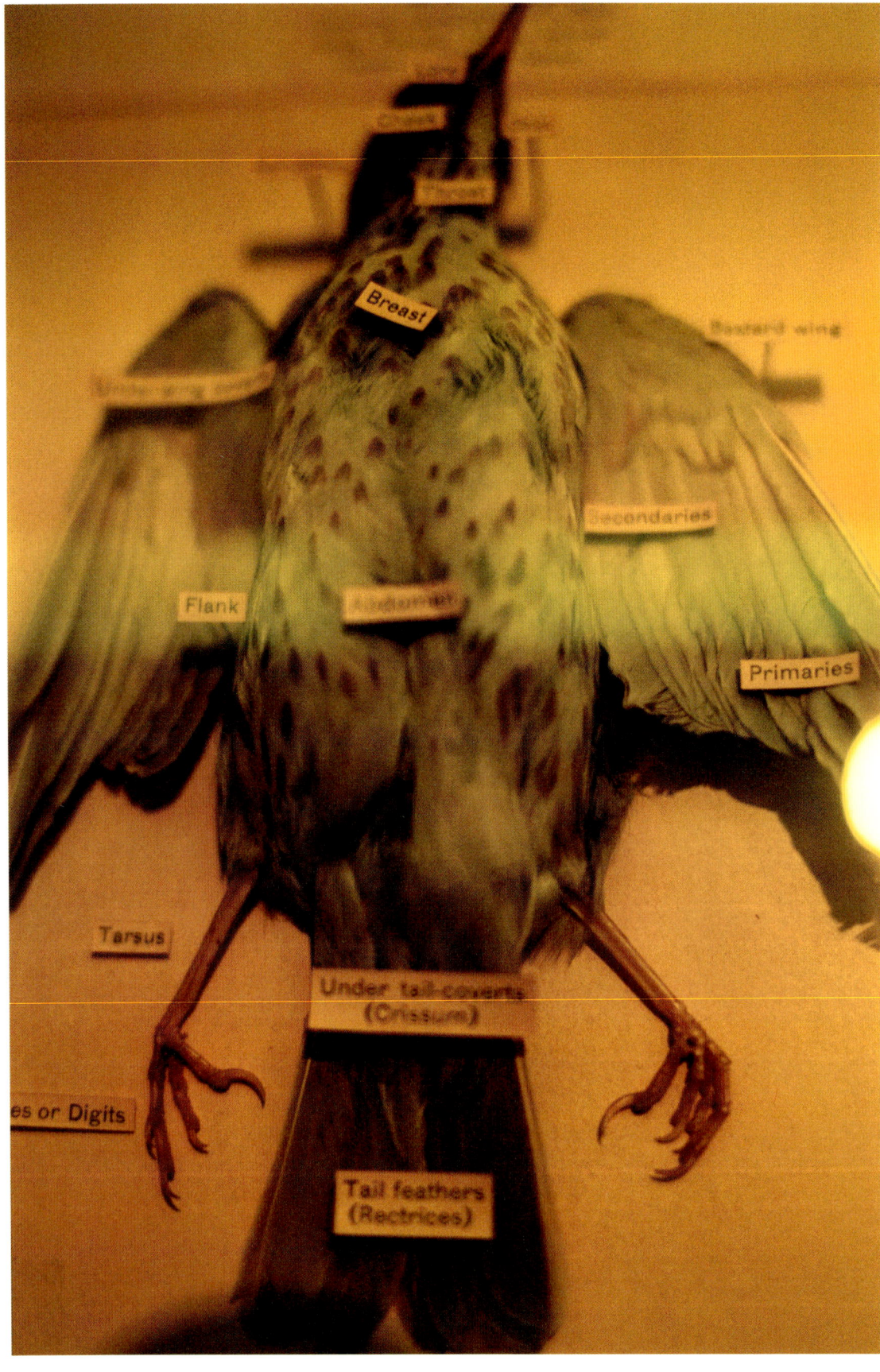

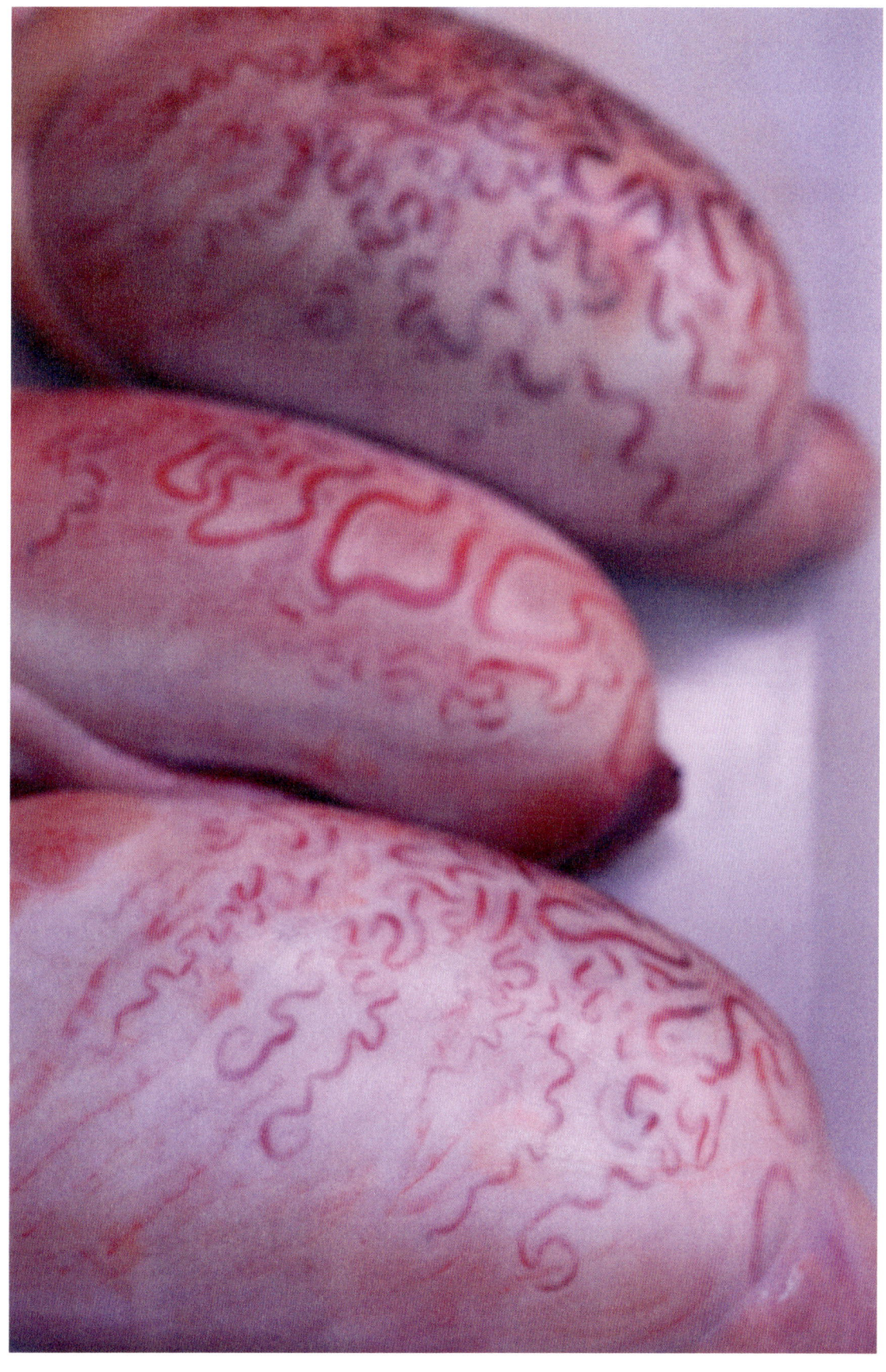

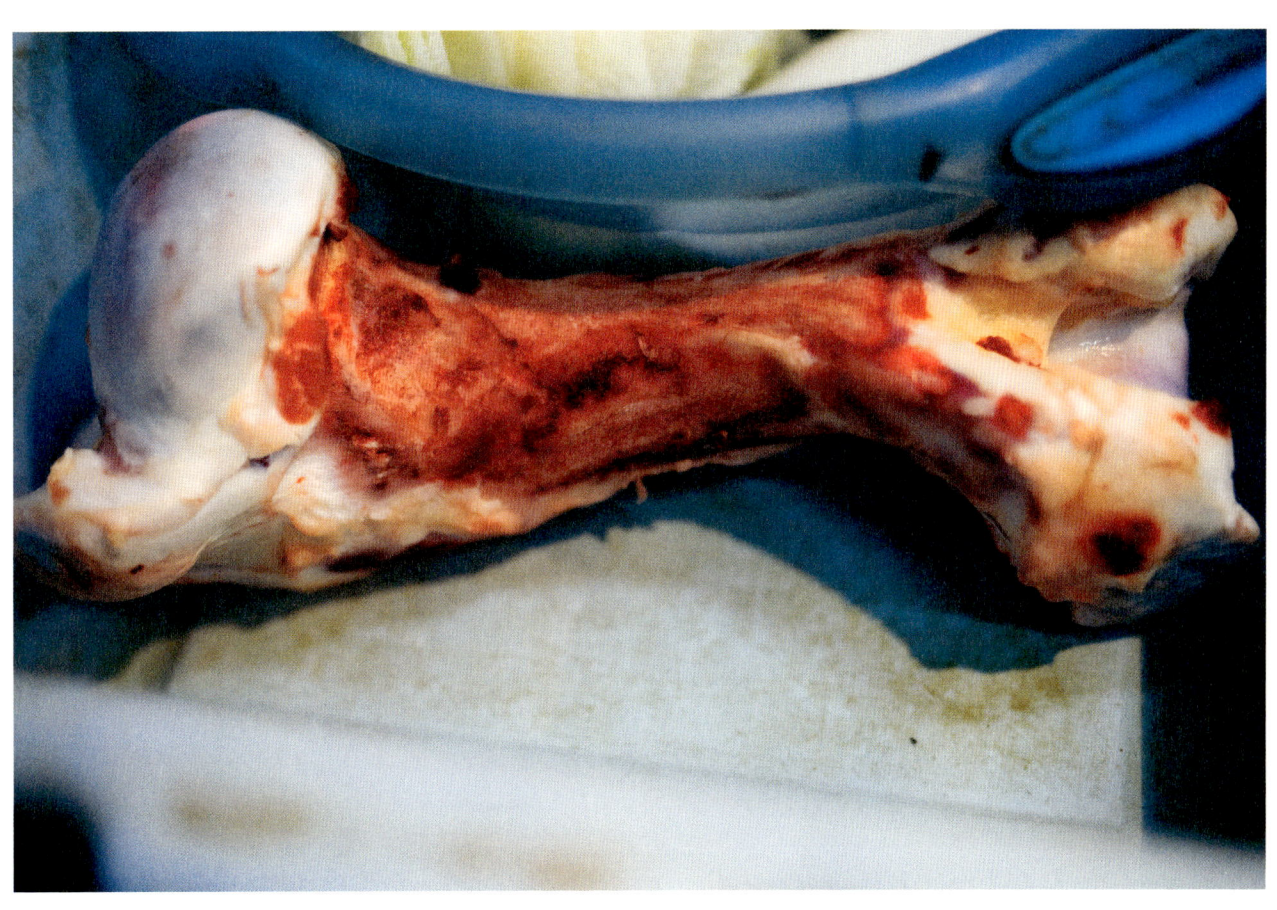

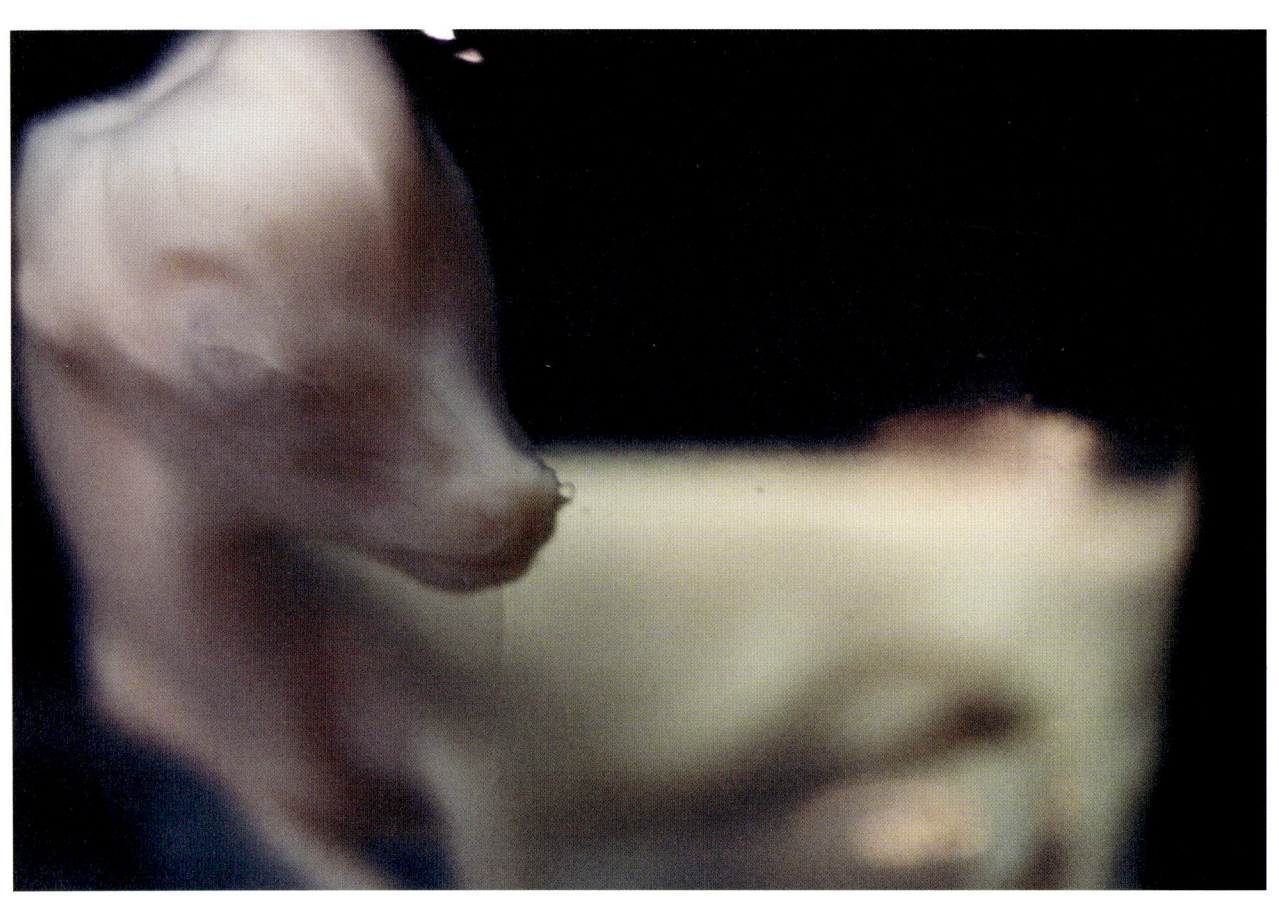

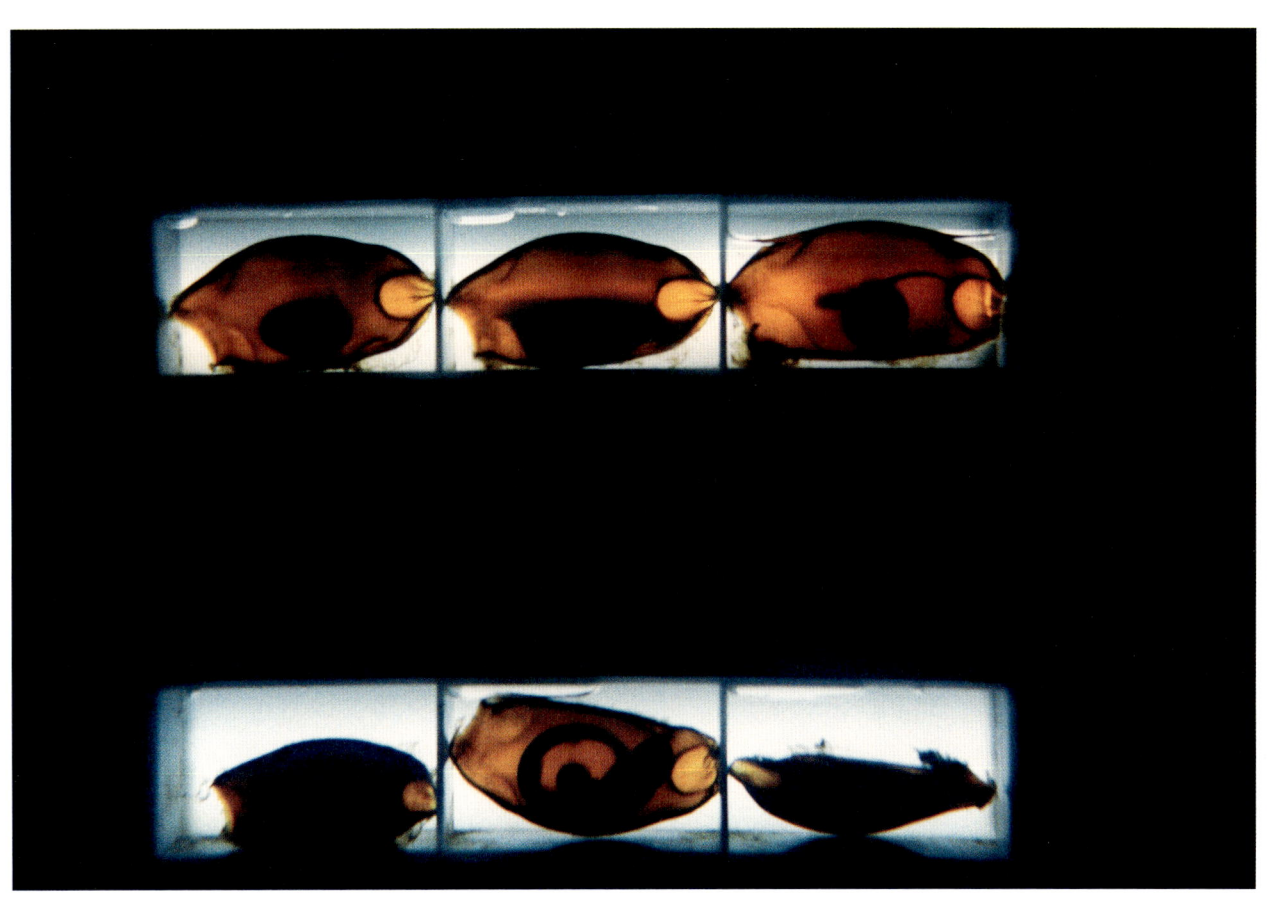

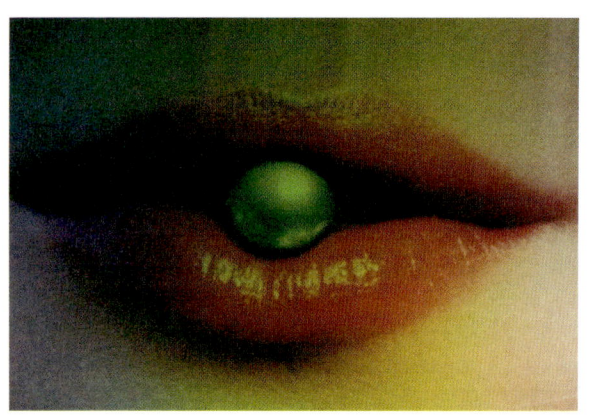 

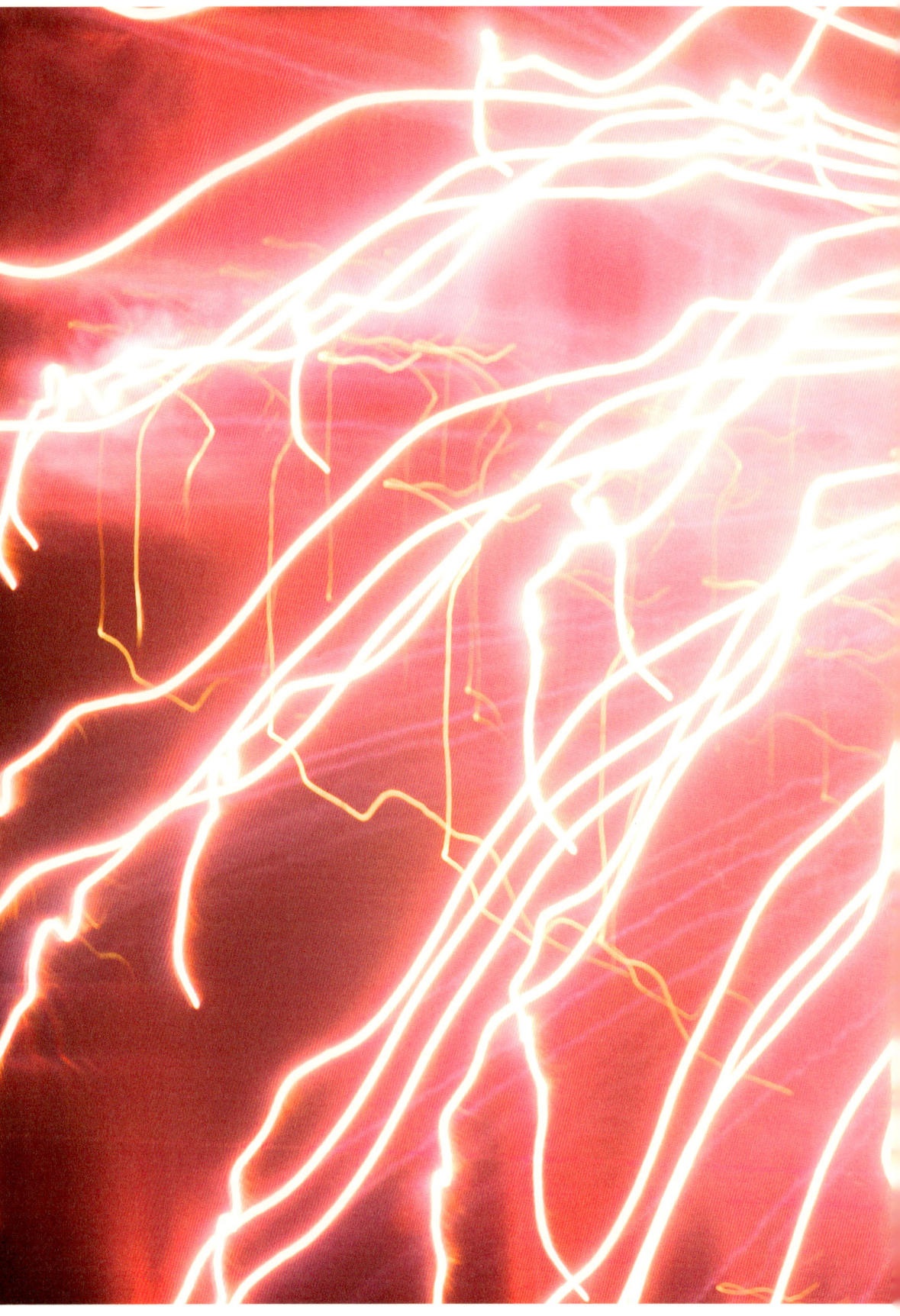

PLANT A TREE

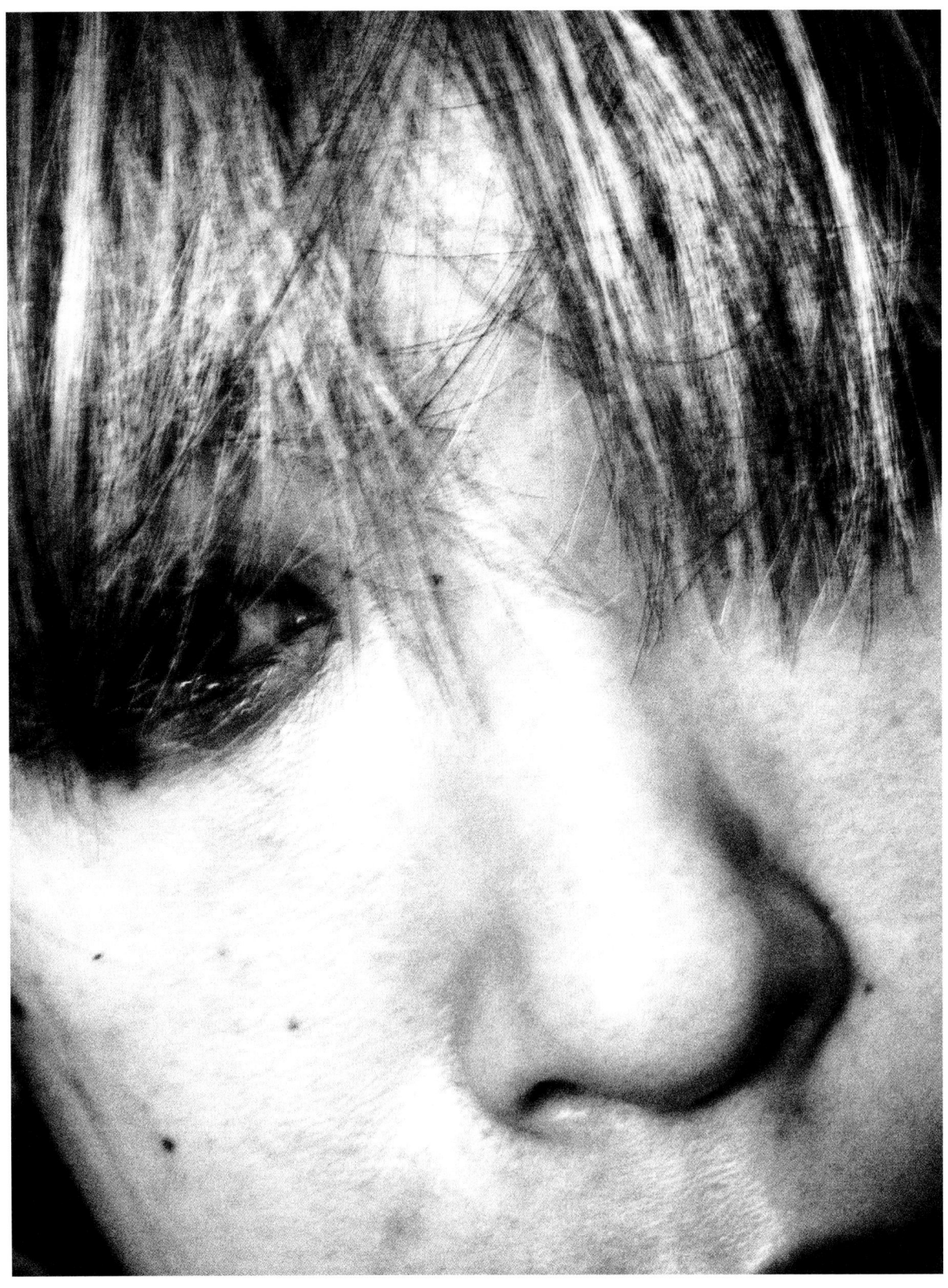

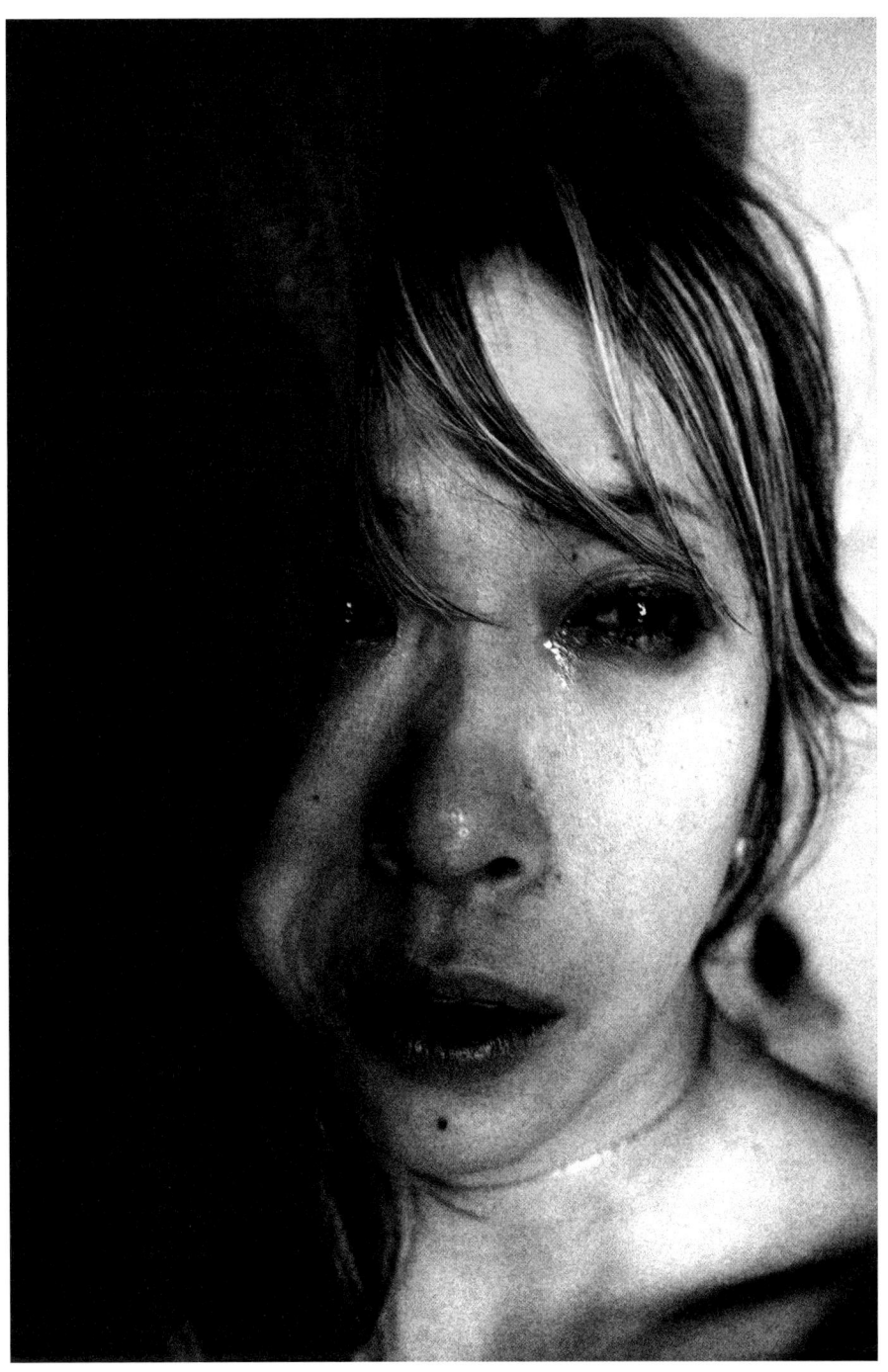

目を凝らせば鬱陶しい程溢れかえっている生とか死とか
黒の中には色が溢れ、色の中に黒は潜む
私達が食するものはあらゆるものの屍
花は枯れながらも咲き乱れ
愛玩動物達は今日も檻の中
新しい生命はひたすら生まれまくり
一日一日死に向かって生き続ける
眩しいくらいに
さあ、行こう
私はこの不感症な日々を精一杯生きる

蜷川実花

If we look closely, we see life and death overflow to a depressing degree
Color overflows within black, black lurks within color
Our food consists of every kind of dead body
Flowers bloom in the midst of dying
Pet animals remain in their cages again today
New life is born with reckless abandon
Continuing to live towards death, day by day
It is almost dazzling
Come on, let's go
I will live every frigid day to its full

Mika Ninagawa

Mika Ninagawa: Self-image

1. Los Angeles, 2012
2. Hong Kong, 2014
3. Hawaii, 2011
4. New York, 2014
5. New York, 2011
6. Tokyo, 2013
7. New York, 2014
8. Tokyo, 2010
9. Tokyo, 2013
10. Cambodia, 2010
11. Rome, 2010
12. Cambodia, 2010
13. Cambodia, 2010
14. New York, 2010
15. Hawaii, 2011
16. Hawaii, 2011
17. Cambodia, 2010
18. Los Angeles, 2012
19. Tokyo, 2010
20. Paris, 2010
21. Tokyo, 2013
22. Paris, 2006
23. Shanghai, 2014
24. Hong Kong, 2009
25. Niigata, 2014
26. Tokyo, 2014
27. Hong Kong, 2009
28. Taiwan, 2011
29. Tokyo, 2014
30. Tokyo, 2014
31. Taiwan, 2009
32. London, 2009
33. Thailand, 2008
34. Shanghai, 2009
35. Bali, 2007
36. Thailand, 2008

37. Chiba, 2014
38. Taiwan, 2011
39. Thailand, 2007
40. Paris, 2012
41. Shanghai, 2013
42. Hong Kong, 2014
43. Hong Kong, 2014
44. Hong Kong, 2014
45. Hong Kong, 2014
46. Hong Kong, 2014
47. Hong Kong, 2014
48. Thailand, 2013
49. London, 2009
50. Ibiza, 2014
51. Cambodia, 2010
52. Paris, 2012
53. Hong Kong, 2005
54. Shanghai, 2011
55. Shanghai, 2007
56. Shanghai, 2010
57. Thailand, 2013
58. Tokyo, 2014
59. Niigata, 2014
60. Belgium, 2013
61. Chiba, 2014
62. Tokyo, 2014
63. Belgium, 2013
64. Belgium, 2013
65. Ibiza, 2014
66. Shanghai, 2007
67. Shanghai, 2009
68. New York, 2007
69. Tokyo, 2012
70. Thailand, 2013
71. Niigata, 2014
72. Paris, 2012
73. New York, 2010

74. Hokkaido, 2010
75. Tokyo, 2012
76. Hong Kong, 2010
77. Chiba, 2014
78. Tokyo, 2010
79. Tokyo, 2010
80. Tokyo, 2010
81. Tokyo, 2010
82. Tokyo, 2010
83. Tokyo, 2010
84. Tokyo, 2010
85. Tokyo, 2010
86. Tokyo, 2010
87. Tokyo, 2010
88. Tokyo, 2010
89. Tokyo, 2010
90. Tokyo, 2010
91. Tokyo, 2010
92. Tokyo, 2010
93. Los Angeles, 2012
94. Los Angeles, 2012
95. Tokyo, 2012
96. Shanghai, 2011
97. Paris, 2010
98. Cambodia, 2010
99. Taiwan, 2010
100. Tokyo, 2013
101. Los Angeles, 2012
102. Tokyo, 2012
103. Paris, 2013
104. New York, 2014
105. Shanghai, 2014
106. Tokyo, 2014
107. Tokyo, 2010
108. Rome, 2010
109. Tokyo, 2014

両極を自由に行き来する——蜷川実花の世界

島田浩太朗［キュレーター、美術批評］

　写真家・蜷川実花は、1996年、多摩美術大学グラフィックデザイン科在学中に「写真ひとつぼ展」でグランプリを受賞し、写真家としてスタートする。原色の世界に目覚め、あの「蜷川カラー」が誕生したのもちょうどその頃である。ポップで鮮やかな色合いとともにアイドルやモデル、花々の輝きを捉えた幻想的な作品世界がポジティヴで開放的と評される一方で、華やかさや幸福感と隣り合わせにある歪みや澱み、衰退の影や死の気配をも同時に捉え続けてきた。本展は観客を蜷川のポップな側面というよりはむしろ、よりパーソナルな「私（＝蜷川実花）」の内面世界へと誘う。写真家・映画監督として世界を忙しく飛びまわる作家に個展「Self-image」について話を聞いた。

　今回の展示は、「Self-image」という展覧会タイトルが示す通り、1996年にセルフポートレートでデビューしてから約20年のあいだに撮り溜めてきたセルフポートレートを中心に構成しています。私はこれまで小さな仕事から映画などの大規模なプロジェクトに至るまで多くの仕事をしてきましたが、最近、ずいぶん贅肉がついてきたなという気がしていました。現場にスタッフがいっぱいいて、スターがいて、ポップで、・・・といった要素を除いても、「私」、まだいけるよね、ということを自分で確認したいという欲求もあるのかもしれませんが、時々、カメラ一台で何でも出来るよね、ということを確認したくなるんです。私の場合、普段から全ての写真を発表することを前提として撮っているわけではなくて、日頃撮り溜めているものの中で「これは面白いな」というものについては、その後、その意味合いを確認しつつ、機会があれば再構成して発表していくというようなスタンスです。とりわけセルフポートレートについては、撮影時に「いつかどこかで発表しよう」という意識が最も希薄です。そして実は初期（1996年頃）と「さくらん」（2007年）と「ヘルタースケルター」（2012年）の時期にしか、セルフポートレートは撮っていません。華やかでコマーシャルな仕事をしていくなかで、「蜷川実花」というイメージが実体から離れて膨張して大きくなっていくことは必ずしも嫌ではないのですが、やはり少し違和感を覚えることがあります。そうした状況のなかにいる時、自分自身のなかでバランスをとるために、やはりどうしてもまったく真逆のことをやりたくなるんです。今回の展覧会は、私のポップではない側面をみんなに見て欲しいなという気持ちがある沸点に達したという感じです。

　蜷川にとって初の美術館での個展「蜷川実花——地上の花、天上の色——」展（2008〜2010年）では、初期のモノクロのセルフポートレート、旅、花、金魚、ポートレート、といったテーマによる、いわゆる回顧展の展示構成で観客の期待にも応えることで、巡回した美術館の一つであった東京オペラシティアートギャラリーでは観客動員記録を塗り替えるほどの反響があった。本展では、前回の最後の部屋でも発表していた身の周りの闇や影の部分に目を向けたシリーズ『noir』（2008年〜）、川面に散る桜を一心不乱に収めた『PLANT A TREE』（2011年）、（『Self-image』にも収録されている写真も含めた）初期から断続的に撮影してきたモノクロームのセルフポートレート、そして新作の映像作品（音楽：渋谷慶一郎、作曲家）によって構成される。

　今回の展覧会を構想する過程で改めて強く感じているのは、やはり私は「すべてを〈一人称〉でやってきた」ということです。これまでも花や風景を撮ってきましたが、どんな時でも常に「私」というのがその中心にありました。今回の展示は、展示室を進んでいくにつれて、少しずつ「私」の内面に入っていくような構成になっています。最初の部屋（ギャラリーI）は3面プロジェクションによる映像インスタレーションで、金魚、人々の影、唇が、少しずつ重なっていくような作品です。金魚は、畸形と畸形を掛け合わせて畸形にして、またさらにそれらを掛け合わせてさらなる畸形をつくる、とい

うように人の鑑賞のためだけに改良され続けてきた生き物です。ものすごく身近な存在でありながら、ものすごく人工的。畸形と畸形を掛け合わせることで、形としては面白くなるのですが、生命体としては弱くなっていく。寿命も短くなったりとか、ちょっと傷ついただけでそこからばい菌が入りやすくなったりとか。ただ人に見る／見られるためだけに改良された生き物で、実際、自然界に戻したら全く生きていけない生命体になってしまっているわけです。そういった事が世の中には沢山あるわけですが、それに対して何も思わずに生きている。私たちがいかに不感症かということに対する違和感が常にあります。その象徴的なモチーフとしての金魚と、街で金魚のようにたゆたっている人々の影、そして欲望の象徴としての唇、それらが混ざってくるような映像に作曲家・渋谷慶一郎さんによる音楽が重なることで、この展覧会の幕開けに相応しい映像インスタレーションになるはずです。

　蜷川は、(このインタヴューのなかで)尊敬する芸術家として19世紀後半の象徴主義を代表する画家オディロン・ルドン（1840〜1916年）を挙げた。ルドンは当時のアカデミー派や印象派にも属さず、目に見えない人間の内面世界を象徴や暗示という方法を用いて視覚化しようと試みた画家の一人で、当初、(後に色彩へと移行していくのだが)同時代の写実主義に基づく印象派の画家たちに囲まれながらも、頑なに黒（noir）の可能性を模索した。フランス美術の偉大なる幻視者であるルドンの黒と色彩、幻想的世界と深い生をめぐる表現と想起は時空を超えて、いまもなお蜷川を勇気づける。

　次の部屋（ギャラリーⅡ）は、通称「noir」と呼んでいます。赤い着色ヒヨコ、檻に入っている猫、標本など、作品集『noir』（2010年）からのイメージを再構成しつつ、たくさんの新しい写真も追加しました。歓喜して自我がなくなるような快楽的な瞬間だけ

を写した花火やフェスの人々の写真もその中のひとつです。爆音が鳴り響いているなかで踊って自我を忘れることはすごく原始的な行為ですが、そこに居る人たちがみんな楽しくて多幸感があるのかというとそういう風にも見えません。逆にみんなが助けを呼んでいるようにも見えたり、あるいはまぶし過ぎて怖かったりとか。物事には何でも多面性があって、ただ単純に音が鳴って踊っているから楽しいということではなくて、そこに居る人たちには様々なバックグラウンドがあって常に複雑さを含んでいると思います。あるいは別の例を挙げるとすれば、たとえばソーセージや肉って、つまり生き物の死体ですよね。ソーセージは腸にミンチした肉を詰めたもので、それを食すってよく考えたら凄いなと思うわけです。子どものお弁当にも必ず入っているくらい、もはやちょっとカワイイもの、ほっこりするような食べ物として認識されています。すごく私たちの生活に身近な存在になっているけど、よく考えたら凄いよねっていう。そういうすごくノイズがあって、猥雑なもののなかで私たちは生活をしている。そうやって生き物を殺して食しているから可哀想だよねというようなことではなくて、その中で生きていけるような強さや、ある指針を自分のなかにどうやって持つかというのが私の全作品を通して表現したいテーマでもあります。

　美術館の二階へと上がる階段踊り場の縦長の大きなモノクロームのステンドグラスも蜷川によるものである。蜷川は「原美術館の建物の造りが独特なので、建物が持っている力と作品の力のあいだのパワーバランスを意識」し、カラーではなく敢えて白黒の透過性フィルムを用いることで、教会のステンドグラスのような荘厳さを避け、訪れた観客がプライベートな記憶の空間に足を踏み入れるような感覚に誘われるような表現を選んだという。

　2階の真ん中の部屋（ギャラリーⅣ）は、写真集「PLANT A TREE」（2011年）からのイメージを再構成しました。これらのイ

メージは3番目の旦那と別れた日に撮った写真です。この時は本当に悲しかったので、もう完全に内面世界に浸っていて、実際は撮影どころではなかったんですが、そういう時に撮る写真はどこか違うはずだと本能的に思って、涙ながらにカメラを持って子連れで目黒川に行って撮った写真です。写真って本当に面白いなと思うのですが、その時の精神状態とか、色んな物が映るんですよ。これはとても私的な作品で、カメラと自分しかいない状態ってこういうことなんだなって思います。おそらくこれだけ見せられても私が撮った写真とは誰もわからないかもしれません。奥の部屋（ギャラリーV）は、写真集『Self-image』（2013年）からのイメージを再構成しました。「Self-image」はこの展覧会のタイトルでもあるのですが、「生身に近い、何も武装していない」自分が映っています。自覚的に無我の境地でポートレート写真を撮り始めるのは、ちょうどデビューした22歳の頃からです。セルフポートレートは自分でファインダーを覗けないので、写真家の欲が出ません。だいたいこの辺りに映るのかなとカメラをセットしてセルフタイマーで撮るので、撮られる側の意識は入りますが、撮る側の自我が入りません。それはセルフポートレートという形式が持っている、かなり象徴的な図式だと思います。撮る時は自分の感度を高める作業だけが重要で、自分の奥底にある感情と、シャッターを押す指だけがダイレクトに繋がっていたら良いなと思っています。頭の中は真っ白な状態なので、これを何かに使うためになんて考えたりしながら撮ることはありません。

　蜷川は、幼い頃から父親（演出家・蜷川幸雄）の書斎で遊び、演劇を見て育った。10歳でカメラを初めて手にした蜷川は、その後の将来を予感させるような（地獄谷の溶岩の上にバービー人形を載せた）写真を撮り始め、やがて太宰治を読みつつも短いスカートを履いて渋谷のセンター街を徘徊するような女子高生へと成長する。「偉大なる両義性のかたまり」とも称されるシェイクスピアの世界のような――両極を自由に行き来する――現在の蜷川スタイルはどのようにして育まれたのだろうか。演劇と父親からの影響について聴いた。

　演劇の影響はかなりあると思います。たとえば、写真を撮る際のセットを組むときの癖ですね。遠景、中景、近景とか。それは凄く演劇的なことが影響していると思います。父の稽古場には行ったことはありませんが、上演は小さな頃から見ていましたし、監視室みたいなところでよく遊んでいました。内容もわからず、眼に焼き付いた光景が沢山あります。おそらく映画を見ている本数より多いと思います。たぶん300本くらいかな。また父からの影響だと、父の書斎で横尾忠則さんの画集や藤原新也さんの本が好きで良く見ていました。家には四谷シモンさんの人形があったり、合田佐和子さんの絵や呪三郎さんのお人形があったりとか。裸にコルセットを着ているような幼女の人形を見ながら、リカちゃん人形で遊んだりしていました。やはりその間に境目がなかったんです。それは未だにそうだと思います。小学校6年のときに丸尾末広のマンガを見つけてビックリしたりとか、そういう経験がいっぱいあります。小さい頃はどちらかというと文学よりもビジュアル的なものを見ていましたが、字が読めるようになってくると父のインタヴュー記事を読むようになりました。父が何を考えていてどのようにものをつくっているのか、ということについてはやはり気になっていました。家では、そういった深いところの話は直接は話さないのですが、父の書籍やテレビのドキュメンタリーとかで読んだり見たりして得た知識や情報と、家の中で見て来た背中とを自分のなかでリンクさせていくという感じでした。それと、小さい頃から本はたくさん読んでいましたが、それは父の書斎からというよりは自発的に色んなもの読んでいました。もちろんマンガも。高校のときは、いわゆる青くさい女子高生だったので太宰治が好きでした。あとは寺山修司とか。でも、同時にギャルだったので、すごく短いスカートを履いて渋谷を徘徊しつつ、太宰治を読んでいまし

た。なんだか今とほぼ一緒ですね。要するに両方を知りたいんです。色んなことがフラットな環境だったと思います。ギャルはこんな本を読まないとかもなく、ミニシアターで映画を観るけど、もちろん合コンにもいく、みたいな高校生でした。

近年、蜷川は映画やミュージックビデオなどの映像作品や、ファッションデザイナーとのコラボレーションなど、ますますその活動の幅を広げている。かつて写真評論家・飯沢耕太郎氏が指摘した「『カメラを持ったシャーマン』とでもいうべき能力」と「写真を通じて観客に『魔法をかける』技術」にもさらに磨きがかかる。「蜷川カラー」を纏った華やかな光に包まれた幻想的な世界と、『noir』や『Self-image』で見せる闇の世界。本展では、その両極のあいだで揺れ動く「私（=蜷川実花）」の「セルフポートレート（=自画像）」を、独特な親密さによって提示してみせた作家に今後の展望について尋ねた。

いま次の映画などをいくつか開発していたりして、色々とやることが大きくなっているように見えるかもしれませんが、まず初めに私が写真家であるということは変わりません。デビューしたときからずっと同じことをしていますね。しつこいんですよ。そして写真に関しては正規の教育を何も受けていないので、まったくの独学でタブーがありません。それが他の写真家たちと異なる部分として、最終的に自分にとってプラスに働いていると思います。最初の頃、ボケてちゃいけないとか、その理由が全然わからなかったし、その後、自分の写真をグッズにしたりしていくことにも全く抵抗がありません。やはり写真の教育を受けてこなかったからこそできることが沢山あるような気がしています。私は撮っていくうちに撮りたい物がかたちになっていくので、次に何を撮っていくのかというようなプランもありません。以前は「（写真家として）これはやっちゃいけない」とか、そういう悩みはないようでいて実はすごくありましたが、40歳過ぎてからはもう何やっても大丈夫と

思えるようになりました。今後はアウトプットの仕方が増えていくかもしれませんが、基本的にはこれからもずっと写真を撮っていく人生だろうなと思います。

元邸宅という原美術館の親密な空間で、蜷川のポップな側面ではない、よりパーソナルな「私（=蜷川実花）」の内面世界へと誘われる「セルフポートレート（=自画像）」の作品群と対峙してどのような感想を持っただろうか。蜷川の写真には「演劇の時間」が流れる。光と闇、過剰さと静けさ、低俗と崇高、見せかけと真実、肯定と否定、生と死。蜷川は両極のあいだで宙づりにされながらも、その裂け目、劇的な一瞬を無心に捉えた無数のイメージによって、観る者を幻想的世界へと引き込み、再現と想起の無限運動をつくりだす。かつて古代ギリシャの哲学者・アリストテレスは『詩学』において詩と歴史を対比させて詩の優位性を主張したが、おそらく蜷川にとってどちらが優位かという議論に興味はないだろう。蜷川の「セルフポートレート（=自画像）」は個別的な出来事を綴った歴史であると同時に、（自身や社会の真理を映し出す）普遍的な事柄を語る詩でもある。蜷川はその両方を知るために写真を撮る。そこに芸術の真理、あるいは神秘を求めるからだ。それは長年ルドンが希求していた「〈精神的なもの〉と〈現実的なもの〉の綜合」[1]と重なる。ところで、ルドンが生きた19世紀末はフロイトやユングが人間の心に関心を持ち、また思想界では科学万能の意識に疑問を投げかけてもいた。どうやら私たちはかなり長いあいだ不感症の日々を生きているようだ。

(1) V. Block, in Exh. Cat: The Hague, 1957

See-sawing Freely Between Two Extremes – the World of Mika Ninagawa

Kotaro Shimada Curator, art critic

In 1996, the photographer Mika Ninagawa, while still a student in the graphic design department at Tama Art University, won the grand prize at the 7th Shashin Hitotsuboten, and with it embarked on her career as a photographer. This was also the time she awoke to the world of primary colors which led to the birth of "Ninagawa Color." There is a positive openness that people see in her dazzling pop colors and the fantasy-like photographic world of celebrity idols, models and flowers in all their brilliance. In contrast to this opulence and sense of happiness is a parallel stream of works in which she captures other aspects such as distortion, stagnation, decline and even death. In this exhibition, viewers are invited to enter the inner world of the "Self" (=Mika Ninagawa), to view another more personal side to Ninagawa's pop. I interviewed the country-hopping photographer and film director about the solo exhibition *Self-image*.

As the title *Self-image* suggests, this exhibition is centered around self-portraits which I have taken off and on for about 20 years, starting with the self-portrait that marked my debut in 1996. During this time, I've done a lot of jobs, from small to larger-scale projects such as movies. But lately it dawned on me that mentally I had gotten quite flabby. At work, I am surrounded by numerous staff, stars and pop elements. But sometimes I get the desire to prove that "me, myself" can survive even without all those things. That even with a single camera everything is still possible. In my case, I don't take pictures with the assumption that everything will be published. My stance is that after I've taken and accumulated a certain number of photos, I take the ones that strike me as interesting, figure out what they mean and if the opportunity arises, organize them into something presentable. This assumption is weakest when I take my self-portraits. In fact, the only times I took self-portraits were early in my career (1996) and during the time I directed *Sakuran* (2007) and *Helter Skelter* (2012). As I go on to do work that is glamorous and commercial, I don't necessarily hate the fact that "Mika Ninagawa" has moved away from and become an inflated and blown up version of the real thing. But I do feel a little uncomfortable about it. Under those circumstances, I feel the need to regain a sense of inner balance by doing something completely opposite. I think the current exhibition represents a desire to show everyone a side of me that is not pop, a desire that had reached the boiling point.

Ninagawa's last solo museum exhibition *Mika Ninagawa : Earthly Flowers, Heavenly Colors (2008)* featured early black-and-white self-portraits, travel scenes, flowers and goldfish motifs in a retrospective structure which met viewers' expectations with great success. It even broke the attendance record at Tokyo Opera City Art Gallery in Tokyo, one of its venues. The show at the Hara Museum includes works from her *noir* series (2008-), a study of darkness and shadows that also appeared in Opera City Art Gallery's last room; her PLANT A TREE series (2011) of cherry blossoms scattered on the surface of rivers created during a period of intense focus; her monochrome self-portraits (including some from the book *Self-image*), created intermittently throughout her career, and a new video work (with music provided by the composer Keiichiro Shibuya).

As I was putting the show together, a very strong feeling came back to me, which was that the first-person "I" was after all the creator of all the works. Till now, I'd taken photographs of flowers and landscapes. It didn't matter when I took them, at the center of them all was my "self." In the present exhibition, the further viewers progress through the galleries, the deeper they enter my inner "self." In the first room (Gallery I) is a video installation consisting of three-screen projections of goldfish, shadows of people and lips that gradually overlap each other. In the case of goldfish, deformity is compounded by deformity to create deformity, which is compounded further by more deformity. It is a creature that has been reshaped solely for the purpose of human appreciation. They are extremely common but extremely artificial. By compounding deformity with deformity, it becomes more interesting as a shape, but weaker as a life form. Its lifespan is shortened as it becomes more susceptible to bacterial infection, even with the slightest of cuts. As an organism that has been improved for the sake of human enjoyment, it is no longer capable of surviving in the real world of nature. There are many cases like this in the world, and we live our lives oblivious to them. I feel a constant discomfort about how frigid we are. Motifs that I use to symbolize this are the goldfish, the shadows of people that float around like goldfish in the city and lips which I use to symbolize desire. They appear to mix together in the video which was scored by the composer Keiichiro Shibuya. I believe this befits the opening of this exhibition.

As an artist that she admires, Ninagawa cited (in this interview) the painter Odilon Redon (1840-1916), a representative Symbolist painter of the last half of the 19th century. Belonging neither to the Academy nor the Impressionists at the time, Redon was a painter who tried to give form to an inner invisible world through the use of symbols and suggestion. He stubbornly pursued the possibilities of black (noir) even though he was surrounded by Impressionist painters who took as their foundation the realism of their day (though they would later pursue color). Without a doubt the black, the color, the fantasy world and the "expression" and "recollection" related to the deep life of Redon – that great seer of French art – transcended time and space to provide encouragement to Ninagawa, which continues even now.

The works in the next room (Gallery II) I refer to as *noir*. Chicks dyed red, a cat in a cage, specimens and others: these images I took from the photo book *noir* (2010), reorganized them for the show and added a number of new works. Of the ones added are photographs of people at a festival or a fireworks show captured at a moment of pleasure, the kind that people get lost in.

Losing one's sense of ego while dancing to explosive music is a very primitive act, but do they look like they are having fun and are in a state of euphoria? It seems to me they aren't. On the contrary, they look as if they are calling for help, or are frightened by the much-too-bright light. There are multiple aspects to everything. It's too simple to assume everyone is having a good time just because of the music and dancing. The people have various backgrounds and complexity is always there. I can give another example, say of sausage or meat, which is to say, the dead carcass of a living thing. Sausage consists of ground meat stuffed into intestinal skins. If you think about eating it, it's pretty amazing. Sausage is something that's always included in a child's lunch box. Everyone sees it as food that is somewhat cute, warm and soft. It's a thing that is extremely familiar and extremely bizarre at the same time. We lead lives that are very noisy and surrounded by vulgar things. One of the themes that I try to express in all of my works is how we can have the strength or inner compass that will allow us to live in the midst of all this, not things like how sad it is to kill living things and eat them.

The large monochrome stained glass in the stairway leading to the second floor is also a work by Ninagawa. In recognition of the unique construction of the Hara Museum's building, she was very conscious of the power balance between the building and the artwork. The artist chose black-and-white transparent film instead of color to avoid the solemnity of stained glass in a church, and to make the visitor feel as if he or she were entering into a space of private memories.

In the second room on the second floor (Gallery IV), I've rearranged images from my photo book *PLANT A TREE* (2011). These are images that I shot on the day I broke up with my third husband. Because I was very sad at the time, I had sunk completely into an inner world. It really wasn't a time for photography, but my instincts told me that photos taken then would be somehow different, and so with tears flowing I went to the banks of the Meguro River with camera and child in hand. The photographs are really interesting, I feel, because they reflect my emotional state at the time and a lot of other things. These are very private photos and they make me think, "so this is how things are when I'm alone with a camera." Probably, if people were shown only these images, they would never guess that I took them. In the last room (Gallery V), I've rearranged images from my photo book *Self-image* (2013). The title of the book is also the title of this show. They are photos of myself that are "close to my raw and unguarded self." It was exactly the time of my debut at age 22 that I started to take portrait photos in a conscious way. The eye of the photographer cannot peer through the finder when taking a self-portrait, so his or her desires do not come into play. The camera is roughly positioned and the shot is taken by self-timer, so consciousness remains on the subject side, but the ego is eliminated on the shooting side. I believe this particular scheme of the self-portrait is a very symbolic one. When I'm shooting, the only important thing for me is to increase my sensitivity. I think it is great when there is a direct link between the emotion that lies deep within me and the finger that presses the shutter. Because the mind is blank, there is no thought of how the image will be used while it is being taken.

Ninagawa grew up playing in the study of her father (theater director Yukio Ninagawa) and watching plays. She got her first camera at the age of 10 and, in a way that seemed to foretell her future, began to take pictures (of a Barbie doll on top of lava at Jigokudani (Hell Valley)). Eventually she became a high school girl, read books by Osamu Dazai, wore short skirts and hung out at Center Street in Shibuya. What kind of upbringing did she have that would lead to her present style, one which see-saws freely between two extremes in a way similar to the world of Shakespeare described as a great mass of ambivalence? I asked Ninagawa about the influence of theater and her prominent father.

I think theater had a considerable influence on me. For example, my habit of constructing a set whenever I shoot, with background, middle ground, foreground, etc. Theatrical elements were a great influence. I didn't go to the rehearsal hall, but I watched stage performances ever since I was young. I used to often play in something like an observation room. I didn't understand a lot of the content, but a great many scenes were etched in my mind. I probably saw more plays than I did movies. Possibly 300 or so. As for my father's influence, I liked the books of Tadanori Yokoo's art and books by Shinya Fujiwara that were in my father's study and used to look at them a lot. We had Simon Yotsuya's dolls in our home, pictures by Sawako Aida and Saburo Noroi's dolls. I would play with a Rika-chan doll while looking at doll figures of naked young girls wearing corsets. There was after all no boundaries between them, and I think there still isn't. When I was in the sixth grade, I discovered the comics of Suehiro Maruo and was really amazed. There were many such experiences. When I was a child, I was drawn more to the visual than the written word. Once I learned how to read, I read my father's interviews. I became interested in what my father thought and how he created things. Although we never spoke directly about these things at home, inside of me the knowledge and information that I picked up in my father's study, from TV documentaries and through reading and looking at things became linked to the image of my father's back at home. I also read a lot of books from an early age. They were things that I read on my own rather than things that were in my father's study. This included manga, of course. I was your typical callow high school girl, so I liked Osamu Dazai and also Shuji Terayama, etc. At the same time, I was a gal[1], which means I wore shockingly short skirts and hung out at Shibuya while I read Osamu Dazai. Why, it's almost the same as now. In other words, I want to know both sides. The environment was flat for a lot of things. I never once had such thoughts as "this kind of book is not read by girls," etc. I was a high school student who went to small art theaters, but also to speed dating events as well, naturally.

Ninagawa's scope of activities has been expanding into various other areas in recent years, for example, movies, music videos and other film projects, and collaborations with fashion designers. These efforts are further refinements of abilities befitting "a shaman with a camera," and techniques that "cast spells on viewers through photographs," quoting the photo critic Kotaro Iizawa. Hers is a fantasy world enveloped in the brilliant light of "Ninagawa Color," and a world of darkness of *noir* and *Self-image*. In this exhibition, Ninagawa presents self-portraits of a "self" that see-saws between these two poles with an inspiring intimacy. I asked the artist about her future outlook.

Developing a number of things, including the next movie, and being involved in a variety of things might make it look like I'm working on a larger scale, but I was a photographer from the start and that hasn't changed. Since my debut, I've done the same thing all along. I'm quite obstinate. Also, I never had a formal education in photography. Being totally self-taught, nothing is taboo. I think that part of me is different from other photographers, and in the end, it works to my advantage. In the beginning, I never knew the reason why a photo couldn't be out of focus, and later, I felt no compunction about making commercial products using my photographs. I feel I am able to do a lot of things exactly because I didn't receive an education in photography. In my case, what I want to photograph takes form as I am shooting. Because of this, what I shoot next follows no plan. It may seem I am unencumbered by such concerns as "you can't do that (as a photographer)," but the fact is that I was to a huge degree. But since turning 40, I feel now it is alright to do anything. The means behind my output might vary and multiply in the future, but I think basically I will always be taking pictures from now and forever.

What feelings do you the viewer have as you stand within the intimate space of a museum that was once a mansion, face-to-face not with Ninagawa's pop side, but her more personal self-portraits that invite you into the artist's inner world of the "self"? Within her photographs flows "theatrical time." Light and dark, excess and tranquility, the vulgar and the sublime, pretense and truth, affirmation and negation, life and death. Even while suspended between two poles, Ninagawa draws the viewer into a fantasy world through countless images that innocently capture the theatrical moment, the chasm between the poles, creating an infinite movement of "reproduction" and "recollection." The ancient Greek philosopher Aristotle in *The Poetics* contrasted history with poetry and proclaimed poetry to be the superior of the two. But then Ninagawa would probably not be interested in such a debate on relative merits. Her self-portraits are at once "history" connected with personal events and "poetry" that speak of universal things (reflecting her own or social truths). Ninagawa takes photos in order to know both. This is because it is there she seeks artistic truth or mystery, which coincides with the "synthesis of the spiritual and the actual" that Redon sought after for many years. Incidentally, during the end of the 19th century when Redon was alive, Freud and Jung were interested in the human psyche and intellectuals were raising doubts about the idea of all-mighty science. Apparently we've been living "frigid days" for quite a long time.

(1) A girl who embodied the unique Japanese teenage female culture and fashion that flourished in and around Shibuya during the 1990s and into the 2000s.

蜷川実花

東京都生まれ

1997　多摩美術大学美術学部グラフィックデザイン学科卒業

受賞歴

1996　「第7回写真『ひとつぼ展』」グランプリ受賞
　　　「第13回キヤノン写真新世紀」優秀賞受賞
1998　「第9回コニカ写真奨励賞」受賞
2001　「第26回木村伊兵衛写真賞」受賞
2006　第13回 VOCA展 2006「大原美術館賞」受賞
2012　「新藤兼人賞銀賞」受賞

主な個展

1997　「Walk3」ガーディアン・ガーデン、東京
1999　「Baby Blue Sky」新宿コニカプラザ、東京
　　　「蜷川実花〈女神の島のクリスマス〉」NADiff、東京
　　　「French kiss」ROCKET、東京
2000　「Pink Rose Suite」ROCKET、東京
　　　「Sugar and Spice」
　　　　代官山フォトギャラリー、東京／タンクギャラリー、大阪　*2001年まで巡回
2001　「まろやかな毒景色」
　　　　パルコギャラリー、東京／名古屋パルコギャラリー、愛知
2002　「MIKA NINAGAWA at ISSEY MIYAKE AOYAMA」
　　　　イッセイミヤケ青山店、東京
　　　「私は海を抱きしめていたい」NADiff、東京
　　　「like a peach」スパイラルガーデン、東京／ラフォーレ松山、愛媛
2003　「Acid bloom #1」ROCKET、東京
　　　「Acid bloom #2」NADiff、東京
　　　「Liquid Dreams」
　　　　パルコミュージアム、東京／名古屋パルコギャラリー、愛知　*2004年まで巡回
2004　「mika over the rainbow」
　　　　ラフォーレミュージアム原宿、東京／HEP HALL、大阪／
　　　　広島パルコ、広島／名古屋タカシマヤ、愛知／三菱地所アルティアム、福岡
　　　「photographs 2001–2004」小山登美夫ギャラリー、東京
　　　「MIKA NINAGAWA 蜷川実花展」TKGY at lammfromm、東京
2005　「MIKA NINAGAWA PHOTO EXHIBITION IN LONDON 2005」
　　　　gallery Eclectic、ロンドン

　　　「floating yesterday」GALLERY SPEAK FOR、東京
2006　「永遠の花 1」トーキョーワンダーサイト渋谷、東京
　　　「永遠の花 2」小山登美夫ギャラリー、東京
2007　「Mika Ninagawa Exhibition」Arndt & Partner、ベルリン
　　　「Mika Ninagawa Photo Exhibition」Colette、パリ
　　　「girls' holiday!」LAPNET SHIP、東京／静岡パルコ、静岡
　　　「CELINE meets Mika Ninagawa」
　　　　伊勢丹新宿店本館1階ザ・ステージ、東京
　　　「永遠の花」ガレリアミーシャ、香川
　　　「NINAGAWA WOMAN」表参道ヒルズ スペース オー、東京
2008　「蜷川妄想劇場」
　　　　パルコファクトリー、東京／札幌パルコ、北海道／
　　　　名古屋パルコ、愛知／仙台パルコ、宮城
　　　「蜷川実花展」Mizuho Oshiro ギャラリー、鹿児島
　　　「Secret Flowers」蜷川実花写真館（京都極楽堂書店）、京都
　　　「Mika Ninagawa」Beijing Art Now Gallery (Shanghai station)、上海
　　　「蜷川実花展 ―地上の花、天上の色―」
　　　　東京オペラシティアートギャラリー、東京／岩手県立美術館、岩手／
　　　　鹿児島県霧島アートの森、鹿児島／西宮市大谷記念美術館、兵庫／
　　　　高知県立美術館、高知　*2010年まで巡回　*図録
　　　「mika ninagawa」Helene Nyborg Contemporary、コペンハーゲン
　　　「蜷川実花 GIFT Goods and Prints @NADiff」NADiff a/p/a/r/t、東京
　　　「EROTIC TEACHER ××× YUKA」
　　　　蜷川実花写真館（京都極楽堂書店）、京都

主なグループ展

2009 「Liquid Dreams」GALERIE PRISKA PASQUER、ケルン
　　　「FLOWER ADDICT」小山登美夫ギャラリー京都、京都
2010 「Liquid Dreams & Acid Bloom」
　　　　Galerie Wouter van Leeuwen、アムステルダム
　　　「ニナガワ・バロック／エクストリーム」NADiff A/P/A/R/T、東京
　　　「FLOWER ADDICT」Mizuho Oshiro ギャラリー、鹿児島
　　　「UMEZZ HOUSE」蜷川実花写真館（京都極楽堂書店）、京都
　　　「Mika Ninagawa for International Rome Film Festival」
　　　　Auditorium Arte, Auditorium Parco della Musica、ローマ
　　　「noir」小山登美夫ギャラリー、東京
　　　Exhibition in conjunction with the RIZZOLI Publication "MIKA NINAGAWA"
　　　　EYE OF GYRE、東京
2011 「蜷川実花写真展：MIKA NINAGAWA」キヤノンギャラリー S、東京
　　　「月刊MEN 向井理」BLD GALLERY、東京
　　　「Flower and Goldfish」MOT / ARTS、台北
　　　「noir & SAKURAN」
　　　　Taiwan International Visual Arts Center (TIVAC)、台北
　　　「森山大道×蜷川実花 展」
　　　　タカ・イシイギャラリー京都、京都／小山登美夫ギャラリー京都、京都
2012 「蜷川実花展」浦添市美術館、沖縄
　　　「桜」ROPPONGI HILLS A/D GALLERY、東京
　　　「PLANT A TREE」小山登美夫ギャラリー、東京
　　　「蜷川実花写真展 ヘルタースケルター」パルコミュージアム、東京
　　　「Mika Ninagawa: noir」
　　　　Galerie Wouter van Leeuwen、アムステルダム
　　　「蜷川実花展」8/ ART GALLERY/ Tomio Koyama Gallery、東京
2013 「NINAGAWA MEN and WOMEN」
　　　　阪急うめだギャラリー、阪急うめだ本店、大阪
　　　「月刊MEN 展」
　　　　札幌パルコ、北海道／札幌宮の森美術館、北海道／
　　　　TABLOID GALLERY、東京／ミオホール、天王寺ミオ、大阪
　　　「蜷川実花写真展 LUCKY STAR NINAGAWA MEN & WOMEN」
　　　　表参道ヒルズ、スペース オー、東京
　　　「Hawaii Paradise by Mika Ninagawa 蜷川実花」
　　　　DFS ギャラリア ワイキキ 1F 特設ギャラリー、ハワイ
　　　「蜷川実花写真展」金津創作の森、福井
　　　「noir」ミゼんふくおかカメラ館、富山
2014 「蜷川実花写真展」フジフイルムスクエア、東京
　　　「TOKYO INNOCENCE」阪急うめだ本店 9 階祝祭広場、大阪
　　　「ETRO × MIKA」ETRO BOUTIQUE LONDON、ロンドン
　　　「Mika Ninagawa」Viborg Kunsthal、ヴィボー、デンマーク
2015 「蜷川実花：Self-image」原美術館、東京 ＊図録
　　　「noir」8/ ART GALLERY/ Tomio Koyama Gallery、東京
　　　「Portraits & Flowers」CAPSULE／SUNDAY、東京

1997 「ネイキッドアイズ」パルコギャラリー、東京
　　　「Japanese New Generation Photographers」Colette、パリ
1999 「水戸アニュアル'99 プライベートルーム II ―新世代の写真表現」
　　　　水戸芸術館現代美術ギャラリー、茨城 ＊図録
2001 「それぞれの部屋：Three Rooms」
　　　　エプソンイメージングギャラリー エプサイト、東京
　　　「第 26 回木村伊兵衛写真賞受賞展」〔長島有里枝／蜷川実花／HIROMIX〕
　　　　新宿ミノルタフォトスペース、東京／大阪ミノルタフォトスペース、大阪／他巡回
2002 「THE ドラえもん展」
　　　　サントリーミュージアム［天保山］、大阪／そごう美術館、神奈川／
　　　　北海道立旭川美術館、北海道／松坂屋美術館、愛知／大分市美術館、大分／
　　　　島根県美術館、島根／秋田市立千秋美術館、秋田／高岡市美術館、富山／
　　　　高松市美術館、香川／松本市美術館、長野／
　　　　長崎県立美術館県民ギャラリー、長崎 ＊2006 年まで巡回 ＊図録
　　　「写真新世紀 10 周年記念展 Futuring Power」
　　　　東京都写真美術館、東京／海岸通ギャラリー・CASO、大阪
　　　「VERSUS EXHIBITION 02 –UK vs JAPAN– 」
　　　　中目黒 DEPOT、東京／パルコミュージアム、東京／
　　　　名古屋パルコギャラリー、愛知 ＊2003 年まで巡回
　　　「平遥国際写真フェスティバル」平遥古城、山西省、中国
2003 「『ひとつぼ展』20 回記念 going 1992-2002」
　　　　ガーディアン・ガーデン、東京 ＊図録
　　　「ぴあ通巻 1000 号記念展 希望／HOPE ―未来は僕等の手の中」
　　　　ラフォーレミュージアム原宿、東京
　　　「日本の新進作家 Vol.2 ―幸福論」東京都写真美術館、東京 ＊図録
　　　「ディズニーグッズ ラボラトリー 東京展」Gallery CLASKA、東京
　　　「take art collection 2003」スパイラルガーデン、東京
　　　「KEEP IN TOUCH: Positions in Japanese Photography」
　　　　Kunsthaus Graz、グラーツ、オーストリア
　　　「第 41 回 岡山市芸術祭 LOVE PLANET ―愛の惑星」
　　　　旧出石小学校教室、岡山
2004 「HARAJUKU COLLABO. APARTMENT 2004」
　　　　ラフォーレミュージアム原宿、東京
　　　「夢みるタカラヅカ展 ～宝塚歌劇に魅了された芸術家、そして時代～」
　　　　サントリーミュージアム［天保山］、大阪／東京オペラシティアートギャラリー、東京／
　　　　そごう美術館、神奈川 ＊図録
2005 「庭園植物記」東京都庭園美術館、東京 ＊図録
　　　「開館記念展 vol. 1 たからもの―写真と言の葉」
　　　　横浜市民ギャラリーあざみ野、神奈川
2006 「VOCA 展 2006 現代美術の展望 ―新しい平面の作家たち―」
　　　　上野の森美術館、東京 ＊図録
　　　「アイドル！」横須賀美術館、神奈川 ＊図録
　　　「魚のすがた展 ―みる、釣る、喰う、祈る、遊ぶ―」
　　　　愛媛県美術館、愛媛 ＊図録

2007	「Tokyo Design Premio 2007 – Tokyo Designer's Week in Milan 2007」
	Superstudio Piu、ミラノ
	『「ひとつぼ」スカラシップ奨学生展』、ガーディアン・ガーデン、東京
	「Gelatin Silver Session 07 展 —Film を次の世代へ残すために—」
	アクシスギャラリー、東京／art project ARTZONE、京都
	「SPACE FOR YOUR FUTURE —アートとデザインの遺伝子を組み替える」
	東京都現代美術館、東京　＊図録
	「Professional Photographer 200 人展」フジフイルムスクエア PHOTO IS、東京
2008	「The Masked Portrait」Marianne Boesky Gallery、ニューヨーク
	「JAPAN! CULTURE + HYPER CULTURE」
	The Kennedy Center、ワシントン D.C.　＊図録
	「Faithful Documents: Japanese Contemporary Photography」
	AKI GALLREY、台北　＊図録
	「JAPAN NOW」Inter Alia Art Company、ソウル
	「Review / Preview – Japanese Photographs」Gallerie Priska Pasquer、ケルン
	「ZOOM ON IN OUT JAPAN」
	Wave Photogallery、ブレーシャ、イタリア　＊図録
	「Gelatin Silver Session 08 展—SAVE THE FILM—」
	アクシスギャラリー、東京／名古屋芸術大学アート&デザインセンター、愛知
2009	「花・風景　モネと現代日本のアーティストたち—大巻伸嗣、蜷川実花、名知聡子—」
	熊本市現代美術館、熊本　＊図録
	「医学と芸術展：生命（いのち）と愛の未来を探る」森美術館、東京　＊図録
2010	「In aller Munde」Museum Villa Rot、ブルグリーデン、ドイツ　＊図録
	「TOKYO VISUALIST」
	National Art Gallery Malaysia、クアラルンプール　＊図録
	「Summer Loves」Huis Marseille – Museum for Photography、アムステルダム
	「Very Fun Park: Contemporary Art from Taiwan, 2010」
	台北 101、台北
	「福島現代美術ビエンナーレ 2010『HANA』」
	福島県文化センター、福島　＊図録
2011	「Art in an Office —印象派・近代日本画から現代絵画まで」
	豊田市美術館、愛知
	「蜷川実花・蜷川宏子 二人展 写真とパッチワーク・キルト、母と娘のコラボレーション」
	石川県政記念しいのき迎賓館、石川／HEP HALL、大阪／
	ラフォーレミュージアム原宿、東京／三菱地所アルティアム、福岡／
	鳥取県立博物館、鳥取　＊2013 年まで巡回
	「JAPANCONGO」
	Le Magasin – Centre National d'Art Contemporain、グルノーブル、フランス／他、巡回
	「Future Pass – From Asia to the World, Collateral Event of the 54th International
	Art Exhibition – la Biennale di Venezia」
	Abbazia di San Gregorio、Palazzo Mangilli-Valmarana、
	ヴェニス／他、巡回　＊図録
	「CAFE in Mito 2011 —かかわりの色いろ」
	水戸芸術館現代美術ギャラリー、茨城　＊図録

2012	「Beauty – Flowers in Contemporary Photography」
	東京アートミュージアム、東京
2013	「シブバル展。」パルコミュージアム、東京
	「Ohara Contemporary」大原美術館分館、工芸・東洋館、岡山
	「十和田市現代美術館 開館 5 周年記念展 vol.1 flowers」
	十和田市現代美術館、中心商店街他、青森
	「アートがあればII —9 人のコレクターによる個人コレクションの場合」
	東京オペラシティ アートギャラリー、東京
	「Ausstellung Daido Moriyama / Mika Ninagawa」
	Kasseler Kunstverein、Fridericianum、カッセル、ドイツ
2014	「マインドフルネス! 高橋コレクション展 決定版 2014」
	名古屋市美術館、愛知　＊図録
	「オオハラ・コンテンポラリー・アット・ムサビ」武蔵野美術大学美術館、東京
	「DOMMUNE University of the Arts – Tokyo Arts Circulation」
	3331Arts Chiyoda、東京
	「日本の写真って何ですか？」I 部、TOKYO PHOTO 2014、東京
	「ヴァンヌーボ×15 人の写真家」株式会社竹尾 見本帖本店、東京
2015	「大野智史、桑久保徹、蜷川実花、福永大介」
	小山登美夫ギャラリー、東京

パブリックコレクション

UBS アートコレクション
熊本市現代美術館
大原美術館
トヨタアートコレクション
スルガ銀行
ジャピゴッツィコレクション
Huis Marseille
高橋コレクション
アマナ フォト コレクション
高松市美術館
ETRO COLLECTION
テルモ株式会社

Mika Ninagawa

Born in Tokyo, Japan

1997 B.F.A., Graphic design, Tama Art University, Tokyo

Awards

1996 Grand Prize at the 7th Shashin Hitotsuboten (3.3m² PHOTOGRAPH)
      The Excellence Award at the 13th Canon New Cosmos of Photography
1998 The 9th Konica Encouragement Award
2001 The 26th Kimura Ihei Award
2006 Ohara Museum of Art Prize, The 13th VOCA 2006
2012 The Silver Prize at the Kaneto Shindo Award

Selected solo exhibitions

1997 *Walk3*, GUARDIAN GARDEN, Tokyo
1999 *Baby Blue Sky*, Shinjuku Konica Plaza, Tokyo
      Christmas at Isla Mujeres, NADiff, Tokyo
      French kiss, ROCKET, Tokyo
2000 *Pink Rose Suite*, ROCKET, Tokyo
      Sugar and Spice, Daikanyama Photo Gallery, Tokyo/
      tank gallery, Osaka *Toured until 2001
2001 *Maroyaka-na-dokugeshiki*, Parco Gallery, Tokyo/ Nagoya Parco Gallery, Aichi
2002 MIKA NINAGAWA at ISSEY MIYAKE AOYAMA, Issei Miyake Store, Aoyama, Tokyo
      Ever Holding My Ocean, NADiff, Tokyo
      like a peach, SPIRAL, Tokyo/ Laforet Museum, Ehime
2003 *Acid bloom #1*, ROCKET, Tokyo
      Acid bloom #2, NADiff, Tokyo
      Liquid Dreams,
      PARCO MUSEUM, Tokyo/ Nagoya Parco Gallery, Aichi *Toured until 2004
2004 *mika over the rainbow*,
      Laforet Museum Harajuku, Tokyo/ HEP HALL, Osaka/
      Hiroshima Parco, Hiroshima/ Nagoya Takashimaya, Aichi/
      ART GALLERY ARTIUM, Fukuoka
      photographs 2001-2004, Tomio Koyama Gallery, Tokyo
      MIKA NINAGAWA Exhibition, TKGY at lammfromm, Tokyo
2005 MIKA NINAGAWA PHOTO EXHIBITION IN LONDON 2005,
      gallery Eclectic, London
      floating yesterday, GALLERY SPEAK FOR, Tokyo
2006 *Everlasting Flowers 1*, Tokyo Wonder Site Shibuya, Tokyo
      Everlasting Flowers 2, Tomio Koyama Gallery, Tokyo
2007 *Mika Ninagawa Exhibition*, Arndt & Partner, Berlin
      Mika Ninagawa Photo Exhibition, Colette, Paris
      girls' holiday!, LAPNET SHIP, Tokyo/ PARCO Shizuoka, Shizuoka
      CELINE meets Mika Ninagawa, The Stage, ISETAN Shinjuku, Tokyo
      Everlasting Flowers, Galleria MICIA, Kagawa
      NINAGAWA WOMAN, Space O, Omotesando Hills, Tokyo
2008 *Mika's daydreaming theater*, PARCO FACTORY, Tokyo/
      Sapporo PARCO, Hokkaido/ Nagoya PARCO, Aichi/ Sendai PARCO, Miyagi
      Mika Ninagawa, Mizuho Oshiro Gallery, Kagoshima
      Secret Flowers, Mika Ninagawa Shashinkan, Kyoto Gokurakudo Bookstore, Kyoto
      Mika Ninagawa, Beijing Art Now Gallery Shanghai, Shanghai
      Mika Ninagawa: Earthly Flowers, Heavenly Colors,
      Tokyo Opera City Art Gallery, Tokyo/ Iwate Museum of Art, Iwate/
      Kirishima Open-Air Museum, Kagoshima/
      Otani Memorial Art Museum Nishinomiya City, Hyogo/
      The Museum of Art, Kochi *Toured until 2010 *catalogue
      mika ninagawa, Helene Nyborg Contemporary, Copenhagen
      Mika Ninagawa GIFT Goods and Prints@NADiff, NADiff a/p/a/r/t, Tokyo
      EROTIC TEACHER ××× YUKA,
      Mika Ninagawa Shashinkan, Kyoto Gokurakudo Bookstore, Kyoto
2009 *Liquid Dreams*, GALERIE PRISKA PASQUER, Cologne
      FLOWER ADDICT, Tomio Koyama Gallery Kyoto, Kyoto

Selected group exhibitions

2010 *Liquid Dreams & Acid Bloom*,
Galerie Wouter van Leeuwen, Amsterdam
NINAGAWA BAROQUE / EXTREME, NADiff A/P/A/R/T, Tokyo
FLOWER ADDICT, Mizuho Oshiro Gallery, Kagoshima
UMEZZ HOUSE,
Mika Ninagawa Shashinkan, Kyoto Gokurakudo Bookstore, Kyoto
Mika Ninagawa for International Rome Film Festival,
Auditorium Arte, Auditorium Parco della Musica, Rome
noir, Tomio Koyama Gallery, Tokyo
Exhibition in conjunction with the RIZZOLI publication 'MIKA NINAGAWA,'
EYE of GYRE, Tokyo *catalogue

2011 *MIKA NINAGAWA*, CANON Gallery S, Tokyo
Gekkan MEN Osamu Mukai, BLD GALLERY, Tokyo
Flower and Goldfish, MOT/ARTS, Taipei
noir & SAKURAN,
Taiwan International Visual Arts Center (TIVAC), Taipei
Daido Moriyama × Mika Ninagawa,
Taka Ishii Gallery Kyoto, Kyoto/ Tomio Koyama Gallery Kyoto, Kyoto

2012 *Mika Ninagawa exhibition*, Urasoe Art Museum, Okinawa
Sakura, Roppongi Hills, A/D GALLERY, Tokyo
PLANT A TREE, Tomio Koyama Gallery, Tokyo
Mika Ninagawa Photo Exhibition Helter Skelter, PARCO Museum, Tokyo
Mika Ninagawa: noir, Galerie Wouter van Leeuwen, Amsterdam
Mika Ninagawa, 8/ ART GALLERY/ Tomio Koyama Gallery, Tokyo

2013 *NINAGAWA MEN and WOMEN*,
Hankyu Umeda Gallery, Hankyu Umeda Main Store, Osaka
Gekkan MEN exhibition,
Sapporo PARCO, Hokkaido/
Miyanomori International Museum of Art, Sapporo, Hokkaido/
TABLOID GALLERY, Tokyo/ Tennoji MIO, Osaka
LUCKY STAR NINAGAWA MEN & WOMEN,
Space O, Omotesando Hills, Tokyo
Hawaii Paradise by Mika Ninagawa,
DFS Galleria Waikiki, 1 Floor Gallery, Hawaii
Mika Ninagawa exhibition, Kanaz Forest of Creation, Fukui
noir, Fukuoka Camera Museum, Toyama

2014 *Mika Ninagawa*, FUJIFILM SQUARE, Tokyo
TOKYO INNOCENCE, 9/F Hankyu Umeda Main Store, Osaka
ETRO × MIKA, ETRO Boutique, London
Mika Ninagawa, Viborg Kunsthal, Viborg, Denmark

2015 *Mika Ninagawa: Self-image*,
Hara Museum of Contemporary Art, Tokyo *catalogue
noir, 8/ ART GALLERY/ Tomio Koyama Gallery, Tokyo
Portraits & Flowers, CAPSULE/SUNDAY, Tokyo

1997 *Naked Eyes*, Parco Gallery, Tokyo
Japanese New Generation Photographers, Colette, Paris

1999 *Mito Annual '99 PRIVATE ROOM II -*
Photography by a New Generation of Women in Japan,
Contemporary Art Gallery, Art Tower Mito, Ibaraki *catalogue

2001 *Three Rooms*, Epson Imaging Gallery epSITE, Tokyo
The 26th Kimura Ihei Photography Award Exhibition
(Yurie Nagashima / Mika Ninagawa / HIROMIX),
Minolta Photo Space Shinjuku, Tokyo/ Minolta Photo Space Osaka, Osaka, etc.

2002 *The Doraemon*,
Suntory Museum of Art, Osaka/ Sogo Museum of Art, Kanagawa/
Hokkaido Asahikawa Museum of Art, Hokkaido/
Matsuzakaya Art Museum, Aichi/ Oita Art Museum, Oita/
Shimane Art Museum, Shimane/ Akita Senshu Museum of Art, Akita/
Takaoka Art Museum, Toyama/ Takamatsu City Museum of Art, Kagawa/
Matsumoto City Museum of Art, Nagano/
Kenmin Gallery, Nagasaki Prefectural Art Museum, Nagasaki
*Toured until 2006 *catalogue
Futuring Power - Canon New Cosmos of Photography 10th Anniversary,
Tokyo Metropolitan Museum of Photography, Tokyo/
Contemporary Art Space Osaka
VERSUS EXHIBITION 02 - UK vs JAPAN -,
Nakameguro DEPOT, Tokyo/ PARCO MUSEUM, Tokyo/
Nagoya PARCO Gallery, Aichi *Toured until 2003
Pingyao International Photography Festival,
Pingyao Gucheng, Shanxi, China

2003 *HITOTSUBOTEN 20th Anniversary: going 1992-2002*,
GUARDIAN GARDEN, Tokyo *catalogue
HOPE: do hope for the future, Laforet Museum Harajuku, Tokyo
On Happiness: Contemporary Japanese Photography,
Tokyo Metropolitan Museum of Photography, Tokyo *catalogue
Disney Goods Laboratory Tokyo, Gallery CLASKA, Tokyo
take art collection 2003, Spiral Garden, Tokyo
KEEP IN TOUCH: Positions in Japanese Photography,
Kunsthaus Graz, Austria
Okayama City Arts Festival 2003 - LOVE PLANET,
former Izushi Elementary School, Okayama

2004 *HARAJUKU COLLABO. APARTMENT 2004*,
Laforet Museum Harajuku, Tokyo
TAKARAZUKA: The Land of Dreams,
Suntory Museum in Tempozan, Osaka/ Tokyo Opera City Art Gallery, Tokyo/
Sogo Museum of Art, Kanagawa *catalogue

2005 *Artists' Gardens - Botanical Recollections*,
Tokyo Metropolitan Teien Art Museum, Tokyo *catalogue

	My Precious: Photos and Words Five Contemporary Japanese Photographers,
	Yokohama Civic Art Gallery Azamino, Kanagawa
2006	*The Vision of Contemporary Art 2006*, The Ueno Royal Museum, Tokyo *catalogue
	Idols, Yokohama Museum of Art, Kanagawa *catalogue
	Fish and our Lives, The Museum of Art, Ehime, *catalogue
2007	*Tokyo Design Premio 2007 - Tokyo Designer's Week in Milan 2007*,
	Superstudio Piu, Milan, Italy
	HITOTSUBO scholarship recipient exhibition, Guardian Garden, Tokyo
	Gelatin Silver Session 07,
	Axis Gallery, Tokyo/ art project room ARTZONE, Kyoto
	SPACE FOR YOUR FUTURE: Recombining the DNA of Art and Design,
	Museum of Contemporary Art Tokyo, Tokyo *catalogue
	200 Professional Photographers Exhibition,
	PHOTO IS, FUJIFILM SQUARE, Tokyo
2008	*The Masked Portrait*, Marianne Boesky Gallery, New York
	JAPAN! CULTURE + HYPER CULTURE,
	The Kennedy Center, Washington D.C. *catalogue
	Faithful Documents: Japanese Contemporary Photography,
	AKI GALLERY, Taipei *catalogue
	JAPAN NOW, Inter Alia Art Company, Seoul
	Review / Preview - Japanese Photographs, Gallerie Priska Pasquer, Cologne
	ZOOM ON IN OUT JAPAN,
	Wave Photogallery, Brescia, Italy *catalogue
	Gelatin Silver Session 08: SAVE THE FILM,
	Axis Gallery, Tokyo/
	Art & Design Center, Nagoya University of Arts, Aichi
2009	*FLOWERS AND LANDSCAPE Claude Monet and Young Japanese Artists:*
	Shinji Ohmaki, Mika Ninagawa, and Satoko Nachi,
	The Contemporary Art Museum, Kumamoto *catalogue
	Medicine and Art: Imagining a Future for Life and Love,
	Mori Art Museum, Tokyo *catalogue
2010	*In aller Munde*, The Museum Villa Rot, Burgrieden, Germany *catalogue
	TOKYO VISUALIST,
	National Art Gallery Malaysia, Kuala Lumpur, Malaysia *catalogue
	Summer Loves,
	Huis Marseille - Museum for Photography, Amsterdam, Netherlands
	Very Fun Park: Contemporary Art from Taiwan, 2010, Taipei 101, Taipei
	HANA: Contemporary Art Biennare of Fukushima 2010,
	Fukushima Prefectural Culture Center, Fukushim *catalogue
2011	*Art in an Office*, Toyota Municipal Museum of Art, Aichi
	Mika & Hiroko NINAGAWA,
	Shiinoki geihinkan, Ishikawa/ HEP HALL, Osaka/
	Laforet Museum, Tokyo/ Mitsubishi-jisho Artium, Fukuoka/
	Tottori Prefectural Museum, Tottori *Toured until 2013

	JAPANCONGO,
	Le Magasin - Centre National d'Art Contemporain, Grenoble, France
	Future Pass - From Asia to the World,
	Collateral Event of the 54th International Art Exhibition - la Biennale di Venezia,
	Abbazia di San Gregorio, Palazzo Mangilli-Valmarana, Venice, Italy *catalogue
	CAFE in Mito 2011: Relationships in Color,
	Contemporary Art Gallery, Art Tower Mito, Ibaraki *catalogue
2012	*Beauty - Flowers in Contemporary Photography*, Tokyo Art Museum, Tokyo
2013	*Shibuparuten*, PARCO Museum, Tokyo
	Ohara Contemporary, Ohara Museum of Art, Okayama
	Towada Art Center 5th Anniversary Exhibition: flowers,
	Towada Art Center, around Central Shopping etc., Aomori
	Why not live for Art? II - 9 collectors reveal their treasures,
	Tokyo Opera City Art Gallery, Tokyo
	Ausstellung Daido Moriyama / Mika Ninagawa,
	Kasseler Kunstverein, Fridericianum, Kassel, Germany
2014	*Takahashi Collection 2014 Mindfulness!*, Nagoya City Art Museum, Aichi *catalogue
	Ohara Contemporary at Musabi, Musashino Art University Museum, Tokyo
	DOMMUNE University of the Arts – Tokyo Arts Circulation –,
	3331 Arts Chiyoda, Tokyo
	What is Japanese Photography?,
	Exhibition Part I, TOKYO PHOTO, Tokyo
	VENT NOUVEAU × 15 Photographers,
	MIHONCHO HONTEN (Takeo Showroom), Tokyo
2015	*Daisuke Fukunaga, Toru Kuwakubo, Mika Ninagawa, Satoshi Ohno*,
	Tomio Koyama Gallery, Tokyo

Public collection

UBS Art Collection
Contemporary Art Museum, Kumamoto
Ohara Museum of Art
Toyota Art Collection
SURUGA BANK
The Japigozzi Collection
Huis Marseille
TAKAHASHI COLLECTION
amana photo collection
Takamatsu City Museum of Art
ETRO COLLECTION
TERUMO CORPORATION

主要文献

主な写真集

- 「17 9 '97」メタローグ、1998年
- 「Baby Blue Sky.」メタローグ、1999年
- 「Sugar and Spice」河出書房新社、2000年
- 「Pink Rose Suite」エディシオン・トレヴィル、2001年
- 「like a peach」講談社、2002年
- 「a piece of heaven」エディシオン・トレヴィル、2002年
- 「Acid Bloom」エディシオン・トレヴィル／ Nazraeli Press、2003年
- 「Liquid Dreams」エディシオン・トレヴィル、2003年
- 「over the rainbow」講談社、2004年
- 「mika」講談社、2004年
- 「プリンセス：栗山千明×蜷川実花」講談社、2004年
- 「floating yesterday」講談社、2005年
- 「永遠の花」小学館、2006年
- 「さくらん写真集」講談社、2007年
- 「しょこたんかんぬ（中川翔子写真集）」ワニブックス、2007年
- 「girls' holiday!」インデックス・コミュニケーションズ、2007年
- 「CELINE meets Mika Ninagawa」CELINE、2007年
- 「蜷川妄想劇場」集英社、2008年
- 「EROTIC TEACHER ××× YUCA」祥伝社、2008年
- 「NINAGAWA WOMAN」講談社、2008年
- 「FLOWER ADDICT」美術出版社、2009年
- 「UMEZZ HOUSE」小学館、2009年
- 「noir」河出書房新社、2010年
- 「MIKA NINAGAWA」Rizzoli New York、2010年
- 「しょこたんかんぬ 2（中川翔子写真集）」ワニブックス、2011年
- 「PLANT A TREE」MATCH and Company、2011年
- 「桜」河出書房新社、2011年
- 「月刊MEN SPECIAL 窪塚洋介 NOWHERE」ポニーキャニオン、2011年
- 「HELTER-SKELTER」パルコ出版、2012年
- 「NINAGAWA WOMAN 2」講談社、2013年
- 「NINAGAWA MEN 1」講談社、2013年
- 「Self-image」MATCH and Company、2013年
- 「TOKYO INNOCENCE」光村推古書院、2013年
- 「脱ぎやがれ！」（大島優子写真集）幻冬舎、2014年

主な逐次刊行物

- 「半生と写真、そのすべて 蜷川実花による蜷川実花」、『美術手帖』美術出版社、915号、2008年11月
- 「蜷川実花」、『文藝別冊』河出書房新社（KAWADE夢ムック）、2009年
- 「特集 蜷川実花 映画『ヘルタースケルター』の世界」、『ユリイカ』、第44巻第7号、2012年7月号

映画

- 『さくらん』制作／蜷川組「さくらん」フィルム・コミッティ、2007年
- 『ヘルター スケルター』制作／映画「ヘルタースケルター」製作委員会、2012年

主な映像作品

- 『Cheap Trip』（mod's hair ショートムービー）監督・撮影、2003年
- rose bullet 2007SS イメージビデオ 監督・撮影、2007年
- 『明日天気になあれ』（ゆず MV）監督、2007年
- WWD × au special fashion shooting 監督・撮影、2008年
- 『涙がこぼれそう』（THE BIRTHDAY MV）監督、2008年
- Cher 15th anniversary film 監督・撮影、2010年
- 『ヘビーローテーション』（AKB48 MV）監督・ジャケット撮影、2010年
- 『SAKURA』（shu uemura ショートムービー）監督・スチール、2011年
- 『ハイチオール B』（エスエス製薬 CM）監督、2011年
- Samantha Thavasa CM 監督・スチール、2011年、2012年
- 『呼び捨てファンタジー』（AKB48 チーム B MV）監督、2011年
- 『ふともも』（FIRE BALL MV）監督、2012年
- 『花火』『Powder Snow ～永遠に終わらない冬～』（三代目 J Soul Brothers MV）監督・ジャケット撮影、2012年
- 『Sugar Rush』（AKB48 MV）監督、2012年
- ピンクスパイダー inspired by バッファロー5人娘（倖田來未 MV）監督・スチール、2013年
- 『Girl On Fire directed by Mika Ninagawa』（Alicia Keys MV）監督、2013年
- 『MAGIC COLOR』（AMIAYA MV）監督・ジャケット撮影、2013年
- 『さよならクロール』（AKB48 MV）監督・ジャケット撮影、2013年
- 『一千一秒』（TAKAHIRO MV）監督・ジャケット撮影、2013年
- 篠田麻里子 卒業映像 監督、2013年
- 『雨のち晴レルヤ』（ゆず MV）監督・ジャケット撮影、2013年
- 『BLEEZE』（GLAY MV）監督・ジャケット撮影、2014年
- 『smile』（BUMP OF CHICKEN ライブ用映像）監督、2014年
- 『A Day with Masami Nagasawa Directed by Mika Ninagawa』（Folli Follie Special movie）監督・スチール、2014年
- 『KAGUYA』（NEWS MV）監督・ジャケット撮影、2015年
- 『さよなら、アリス』（Flower MV）監督、2015年

謝辞

本展開催にあたり、ご協力とご助力を賜りました関係者ならびに協力機関各位に深く感謝の意を表します。

株式会社ルミネ
ドイツ銀行グループ
ガトーフェスタ ハラダ
小山登美夫ギャラリー
有限会社ラッキースター
ペリエ ジュエ
富士フイルムイメージングシステムズ株式会社
東京リスマチック株式会社
王子エフテックス株式会社
図書印刷株式会社
渋谷慶一郎
evala
ZUMI
sonihouse

株式会社光和
株式会社東京スタデオ
島田浩太朗
清水 穣
蜷川幸雄
町口 覚

（順不同・敬称略）

Acknowledgement

We would like to express our deepest gratitude to the following people and organizations who have given us their generous assistance.

LUMINE Co., Ltd.
Deutsche Bank Group
GATEAU FESTA HARADA
Tomio Koyama Gallery
Lucky Star Co., Ltd.
Perrier-Jouët
FUJIFILM Imaging Systems Co., Ltd.
TOKYO Lithmatic Corporation
Oji F-Tex Co., Ltd.
TOSHO Printing Co., Ltd.
Keiichiro Shibuya
evala
ZUMI
sonihouse

KOWA Co., Ltd.
TOKYO STUDIO CO., LTD
Kotaro Shimada
Minoru Shimizu
Yukio Ninagawa
Satoshi Machiguchi

wa: Self-image

January 24 – May 10, 2015

Hara Museum of Contemporary Art

Selected Bibliography

Selected photo books

17 9 '97, Metalogue, 1998
Baby Blue Sky., Metalogue, 1999
Sugar and Spice, KAWADE SHOBO SHINSHA, 2000
Pink Rose Suite, Éditions Treville, 2001
like a peach, KODANSHA, 2002
a piece of heaven, Éditions Treville, 2002
Acid Bloom, Éditions Treville/ Nazraeli Press, 2003
Liquid Dreams, Éditions Treville, 2003
over the rainbow, KODANSHA, 2004
mika, KODANSHA, 2004
princess: Chiaki kuriyama × Mika Ninagawa, KODANSHA, 2004
floating yesterday, KODANSHA, 2005
Everlasting Flowers, SHOGAKUKAN, 2006
Sakuran, KODANSHA, 2007
SHOKOL et MIKANNE (Shoko Nakagawa photo book), WANI BOOKS, 2007
girls' holiday!, Index Communications, 2007
CELINE meets Mika Ninagawa, CELINE, 2007
mika's daydreaming theater, SHUEISHA, 2008
EROTIC TEACHER ××× YUCA, SHODENSHA, 2008
NINAGAWA WOMAN, KODANSHA, 2008
FLOWER ADDICT, BIJUTSU SHUPPAN-SHA, 2009
UMEZZ HOUSE, SHOGAKUKAN, 2009
noir, KAWADE SHOBO SHINSHA, 2010
MIKA NINAGAWA, Rizzoli New York, 2010
SHOKOL et MIKANNE 2 (Shoko Nakagawa photo book), WANI BOOKS, 2011
PLANT A TREE, MATCH and Company, 2011
Sakura, KAWADE SHOBO SHINSHA, 2011
Gekkan MEN SPECIAL Kubozuka Yosuke NOWHERE, PONY CANYON, 2011
HELTER-SKELTER, PARCO Publishing, 2012
NINAGAWA WOMAN 2, KODANSHA, 2013
NINAGAWA MEN 1, KODANSHA, 2013
Self-image, MATCH and Company, 2013
TOKYO INNOCENCE, MITSUMURA SUIKO SHOIN, 2013
Nugiyagare! (Yuko Oshima photo book), GENTOSHA, 2014

Selected magazines

Mika Ninagawa: BY HERSELF, Bijutsutecho, BIJUTSU SHUPPAN-SHA, no. 915, November 2008
Mika Ninagawa, Bungei Bessatsu, KAWADE Yume Mook, KAWADE SHOBO SHINSHA, 2009
Special issue: Mika Ninagawa - The World of Helter Skelter,
EUREKA, Seidosha, vol.44-7 July, 2012

Films

Sakuran, 2007
Helter Skelter, 2012

Selected movie works

mod's hair "Cheap Trip" short movie (director, cinematography), 2003
rose bullet 2007SS (director, cinematography), 2007
Yuzu "Ashita-tenki-ni-naare" MV (director), 2007
WWD × au special fashion shooting (director, cinematography), 2008
THE BIRTHDAY "Namida-ga-koboresou" MV (director), 2008
Cher 15th anniversary film (director, cinematography), 2010
AKB48 "Heavy Rotation" MV (director, CD cover shoot), 2010
shu uemura "SAKURA" short movie (director, still imagery), 2011
SSP CO., LTD. "HYTHIOL B" CM (director), 2011
Samantha Thavasa CM (director, still imagery), 2011, 2012
AKB48 Team B "Yobisute-fantasy" MV (director), 2011
FIRE BALL "FUTOMOMO" MV (director), 2012
Sandaime J Soul Brothers "Hanabi" "Powder Snow-Eien-ni-owaranaifuyu-" MV (director, CD cover shoot), 2012
AKB48 "Sugar Rush" MV (director), 2012
Koda Kumi "Pink Spider inspired by Buffalo 5 nin-musume" MV (director, still imagery), 2013
Alicia Keys "Girl On Fire directed by Mika Ninagawa" MV (director), 2013
AMIAYA "MAGIC COLOR" MV (director, CD cover shoot), 2013
AKB48 "Sayonara Crawl" MV (director, CD cover shoot), 2013
TAKAHIRO "Issen-ichibyou" MV (director, CD cover shoot), 2013
Mariko Shinoda graduation video (director), 2013
Yuzu "Ame-nochi-hareruya" MV (director, CD cover shoot), 2013
GLAY "BLEEZE" MV (director, CD cover shoot), 2014
BUMP OF CHICKEN "smile" video for concert (director), 2014
Folli Follie "A Day with Masami Nagasawa Directed by Mika Ninagawa" (director, still imagery), 2014
NEWS "KAGUYA" MV (director, CD cover shoot), 2015
Flower "Sayonara, Alice" MV (director), 2015

本書は、下記展覧会の開催にあたり刊行するものである。

【展覧会】　「蜷川実花：Self-image」
　　　　　　会期：2015年1月24日（土）− 5月10日（日）
　　　　　　主催・会場：原美術館
　　　　　　協賛：株式会社ルミネ、ドイツ銀行グループ、ガトーフェスタ ハラダ
　　　　　　企画協力：小山登美夫ギャラリー、有限会社ラッキースター
　　　　　　協力：ペリエ ジュエ、富士フイルムイメージングシステムズ株式会社、東京リスマチック株式会社
　　　　　　　　　王子エフテックス株式会社、図書印刷株式会社、渋谷慶一郎、evala、ZUMI
　　　　　　機材協力：sonihouse

【図　録】　発行・編集：原美術館、株式会社マッチアンドカンパニー
　　　　　　発売：株式会社 bookshop M
　　　　　　造本：町口 覚
　　　　　　英訳：ノーマン チャン、マリナ トコロ（P.7）、ギャビン フルー（P.118）
　　　　　　展示風景写真撮影：木奥恵三
　　　　　　用紙：王子エフテックス株式会社
　　　　　　表紙表面加工：株式会社太陽堂成晃社
　　　　　　印刷・製本：図書印刷株式会社

　　　　　　2015年3月11日 初版発行　©蜷川実花　©原美術館　©株式会社マッチアンドカンパニー

　　　　　　原美術館　〒140-0001 東京都品川区北品川 4-7-25　Tel: 03-3445-0651（代）
　　　　　　株式会社マッチアンドカンパニー　〒107-0062 東京都港区南青山 2-8-2-601　Tel: 03-3470-6423（代）
　　　　　　ISBN: 978-4-908114-00-7 C0072　※掲載作品の著作権は作者に帰属する。無断転載を禁ず。

This catalogue was published on the occasion of the following exhibition.

<Exhibition>　*Mika Ninagawa: Self-image*
　　　　　　Date: January 24 (Saturday) – May 10 (Sunday), 2015
　　　　　　Place: Hara Museum of Contemporary Art
　　　　　　Organized by: Hara Museum of Contemporary Art
　　　　　　Sponsored by: LUMINE Co., Ltd., Deutsche Bank Group, GATEAU FESTA HARADA
　　　　　　Cooperation provided by: Tomio Koyama Gallery, Lucky Star Co., Ltd.
　　　　　　Additional cooperation provided by: Perrier-Jouët, FUJIFILM Imaging Systems Co., Ltd., TOKYO Lithmatic Corporation,
　　　　　　　　Oji F-Tex Co., Ltd., TOSHO Printing Co., Ltd., Keiichiro Shibuya, evala, ZUMI
　　　　　　Equipment support provided by: sonihouse

<Catalogue>　Published and edited by: Hara Museum of Contemporary Art, MATCH and Company Co., Ltd.
　　　　　　Distributed by: bookshop M Co., Ltd.
　　　　　　Book designed by: Satoshi Machiguchi
　　　　　　English translation by: Norman Chan, Marina Tokoro (P.7), Gavin Frew (P.118)
　　　　　　Installation view by: Keizo Kioku
　　　　　　Paper manufactured by: Oji F-Tex Co., Ltd.
　　　　　　Special cover lamination by: TAIYODOSEIKOSHA Co., Ltd.
　　　　　　Printed and bound in Japan by: TOSHO Printing Co,. Ltd.

　　　　　　Published on March 11, 2015　©mika ninagawa　©Hara Museum of Contemporary Art　©MATCH and Company Co., Ltd.

　　　　　　Hara Museum of Contemporary Art　4-7-25 Kitashinagawa, Shinagawa-ku, Tokyo 140-0001, Japan　Tel: +81(0)3-3445-0651
　　　　　　http://www.haramuseum.or.jp　http://mobile.haramuseum.or.jp　http://www.art-it.asia/u/HaraMuseum　http://twitter.com/haramuseum

　　　　　　MATCH and Company Co., Ltd.　2-8-2 #601 Minamiaoyama, Minato-ku, Tokyo 107-0062, Japan　Tel: +81(0)3-3470-6423
　　　　　　http://www.matchandcompany.com　http://bookshop-m.com

　　　　　　ISBN: 978-4-908114-00-7 C0072　All rights reserved.